— Season 1 —

What Now

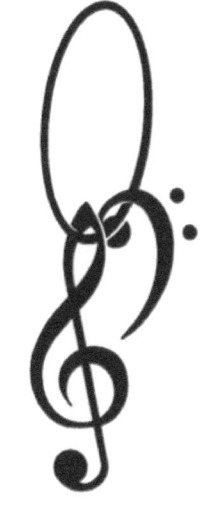

with Simo

by SIMO SAKARI AALTONEN

For a future reader

and my friends Robin Bradley

and Logan L. Masterson

With their passing life got lonelier

They never judged or abandoned me

I wish you guys were still here

"O stay and hear, your true love's coming,

That can sing both high and low."

—Feste in Shakespeare's *Twelfth Night*, Act II Scene 3

Contents

A podcast more like a relaxed late-night radio programme — The title — Experimentation — My situation with regard to the epidemic — Trip to Iceland — Leaving a more lasting and meaningful legacy — Hearing a person's voice — Ray Bradbury — Target audience and not — The only thing we can offer — What makes a person beautiful — Being yourself — My way of expressing myself — We can never know — What will remain — We are all part of this — Becoming more myself — Opening up and speaking from the heart — Getting good practice — The logo — Clefs — Keys — These symbols — From the highest to the lowest — Music — *An Iceland Symphony* — Putting the pieces together — Summing up the symbol — To future listeners — Perfection as an enemy — More on my current situation — Flight — Still a little time left — Intuitive choices — Our own things — Change of scenery — Iceland and Icelanders — Ambient sounds — Unexamined assumptions — Traffic and rain on windowpanes — The chair creaked — Overprocessing — Texture — If you eliminate the record crackle — Crackle of a fireplace — Dream home — Words of encouragement — We will have the world again one day — This is how we grow as people — Absence makes the heart

Contents

grow fonder — My coming quarantine — Thinking of my friends
— Good wishes — A Shakespeare sonnet

Krónur — My time in Iceland growing short — Weather report —
Stronger measures — Brief episode — Travel preparations —
Criminals asked to kindly cancel their plans — *Iceland Monitor* —
Dame Vera Lynn at 103 — "We'll Meet Again" — Some perspective
on our situation — Value of awareness of history — Gratitude for
our devices now — The freedom I've given myself —
Recommendations — Comedy is important — Norm Macdonald
— Interviews, appearances on talk shows, YouTube — Making me
laugh and also making me smile — A really good heart — Jokes
about painful subjects — Relieving a painful tension — Stand-up
about the coronavirus — Natural comedian — Many comedians
exhausting after even a few minutes — Ray Bradbury: "All
Summer in a Day" — Beautiful TV adaptation (1982) — If it
doesn't make you feel something — No hard sell — The ending
even more beautiful — A story told from the perspective of a
young girl — An isolated experience — Perspective —
Remembering the important things in life

Pronouncing my name — No call for dinner — Pass the salt —
Finnish consonants — Day 1 of quarantine — Journey back to

Everything builds on what went before — The years we learn to socialise — Nerd background — *Knight Rider* featuring David Hasselhoff — Drawing comic book adaptations — A talking car with many safety features and that could drive itself — Disney comics popular in Finland — KITT features already a reality — All kinds of comics — Marvel, DC, *Asterix*, *Peanuts*, etc. — Computer games — Game magazines — Newsfield magazine *Zzap! 64* — Original *Star Trek* on a portable black-and-white TV set — Firing the imagination — New *Star Treks* not for me — The more you fill in detail in a story — Daydreaming — No room to imagine anything — More like a theatre play — Just enough detail and nuance — Sets like theatre sets — Love of theatre — Prefer stories where there is stuff left to imagine — Endless roleplaying sourcebook — Working to escape the introverted lifestyle — London last year — Living alone not by choice — Ideal life — Activities when younger — Outdoors adventures and exploring — Rollerskating at 4 a.m. in the Finnish summer — Fresh morning air — Sweden, Iceland, Paris, London, Sidcup — Most friends far away — Watching TV and films with others — A social experience — Missing that — YouTube, Norm Macdonald, *Curb Your Enthusiasm* — Larry David — The relationship of *Curb Your Enthusiasm* to *Seinfeld* comparable to that of season 3 of *Twin Peaks* to the first two seasons — Heightened and extreme — Many other directors than David Lynch involved in the first two seasons of *Twin Peaks* — A healthy form of anxiety — Also the light and the humour — Scenes between Larry David and Richard Lewis — No

— Perfect last couple of lines — "Bless your heart" — Mr. Olmos
on *Miami Vice* and *Battlestar Galactica* — Creative control

My first audio message from a listener — Jumping from one topic
to another — Writing — Day 7 of 14 — Maren's message — Social
interaction — Article on autism — Different possible origins of
problems in social interaction — Sorting and processing
information — Behaviours that resemble autism — Sensory input
— Asperger's — Lack of practice — Autism spectrum — Not fixed
in stone — Studied some psychology — Personal relevance of
these questions — Interacting on our own — Conscious changes —
Looking into this with doctors — An impactful event — May or
may not have had an effect — MRI — Becoming more extroverted
again — Great changes — Eye contact — Used to think more
rigidly — Nothing was impossible to change — We keep changing
throughout our lives — Importance of deciding to change and
believing in it — Unhappiness coming from rigid thinking —
Sympathy for others — The change can only come from within — I
hate manipulation — With most things no clear right or wrong —
No one knows everything — Aiming for happier times

6th April 2020 — A short break — Working on my music — Paris
— Starting my personal system — Day 11 of 14 — About my

odyssey through the history of recorded music — *Gramophone* magazine (founded 1923) used to cover all types of music — Digital archive — Spotify — Widening musical interests from the 80s to the present — *Atlantis* series of games from Cryo — World music — Pierre Estève and Stéphane Picq — Sounds of different cultures — Delving into classical music — *BBC Music Magazine* (founded 1992) — Years focused on writing — Samuel Barber's *Adagio for Strings* — Oliver Stone and David Lynch on using that piece in their films — *The Elephant Man* — National Public Radio recording from the early 2000s — *Platoon* — *NPR 100*: "Barber's *Adagio for Strings*" (9 minutes) — "As Time Goes By" from *Casablanca* (1942) — Many versions of the same songs — Quote from a soldier in World War II about hearing Mozart's *Eine kleine Nachtmusik* — Our situation vs. theirs back then — Beauty hurting and healing — All the music of the world — Perspective — Good wishes

1.9 *Last Day, Pekar, and Keys* (12:34)

9th April 2020 — Day of the Finnish language — Quarantine ending — Thinking of friends — Took a walk — Harvey Pekar and his comic book *American Splendor* — Pekar's appearances on Letterman — He chronicled his own life in comic book form — Now many of us do it online — Pekar made a living as a file clerk at a veterans' hospital — Letterman's later regrets — Made fun of Pekar — Each provoked the other — Pekar's very honest attitude — Refreshing — Great film (2003) based on his comics — Growing respect — May or may not read one day — Look forward to seeing the film — The variety of Letterman's guests — Spending time with someone else a precious gift — Keys to creativity — Creative people talking about creativity — Ray Bradbury, Philip Glass, John Cage, Edward James Olmos, Paul Chadwick (creator of *Concrete*), others — Sparks of inspiration — Messages welcome — All the best

Reading of H. P. Lovecraft's "Ex Oblivione" (1920–1921).

Positive feedback — Aiming this time for no segues — A lot on my mind — More on keys of creativity — Key figures David Lynch, Vangelis, Ron Jones — Interviews, talks, and conversations — Insights — Saying enough but not too much — Vangelis recommendation — Not a marketable commodity — Healthier and wiser — Things that restrict us and things that unlock something — Segue — About creative people I know — So much potential but maybe giving up — Friends or family discouraging — On a more concrete note — Make your own opportunities — Ditch anyone who tries to make you feel worthless — Two-faced people — Another segue — Beautiful accents — Icelandic and English — Used to aim to sound like a native speaker, not anymore — The only thing we have to share — Simple language can be more lyrical, evocative, and expressive — Norm Macdonald's use of

W. P. Kinsella — Featuring Kevin Costner — A few years ago someone asked me who my favourite actor was — The question took me by surprise — More a matter of the story than any actor — Edward James Olmos, Christopher Walken — No good answer — Hero stuff — This most unassuming form of heroism — A lot of people do things for the wrong reasons — Narcissism, desire to impress — The people who simply keep life going — No living under a dark cloud — Ray Kinsella — A humility and gratitude at what he has in life — The greatest treasure a person can have — Working through his issues — The emotional core of this film — The pain of having said something you regret — Too late — A story of a second chance — Humanity and genuine feeling — Another facet of that diamond-hard pain — Parents go through literal trauma in raising a family — The price they pay — The very least we can do — Exceptionally beautiful soundtrack by James Horner — When he was asked to score it — Speechless — Simplicity and taking its cue from the film itself — A big symphonic score would have been all wrong — Appropriate music — A fascinating thing about writing film music — The greatest people — A crazy and unexpected time — Beacons of sanity

A motorcycle — Sunny day — Continuing the serial — I hate manipulation — Playing games with people — Relevance to *Field of Dreams* — Simply a good man — Superman is meant to be a completely goodhearted person — His backstory — From another planet, but raised by really good people — A valuable concept — Many writers don't know what to do with this — Moving on — The connecting link — Whether you can trust someone or not — People reveal themselves over time — Assumptions can be telling — Nearly every superhero ends up being a compromised conception — A more innocent time in comics — Ray Kinsella (Kevin Costner's character) would not crumble — Not violent — Rarer than we may realise — How much happens behind closed doors — A line in an early Sherlock Holmes story — Watson, Holmes, and the countryside — Sherlock has no romantic conception of the countryside — There terrible deeds can continue year after year undetected and unsuspected — Isolated places — Abuse — Real life — Circling back to *Field of Dreams* — A sunny film — Moving — Also scenes of twilight — The word "magical" — Interlude — The people who keep life going may also feel broken — Doing it regardless — Appreciating comedians and the ways they help — Norm Macdonald — Everyone has both dark and light sides — Anything that makes you feel more normal in a bad situation — Do I feel whole or completely together? — Isolation and loneliness are not what a human life is supposed to be — Everyone more or less breaks down at some point — Let it happen — Bending so as not to break — The limit of Ray's aggression — Strength can often be found in unexpected places — One thing sure to worsen depression or anxiety — The real heroes — The unassuming and non-underlined nobility of the main character — Ray and his wife Annie grew up in the 60s — Part of

Introduction

A freeform, wide-ranging podcast on any topics foremost on the host's mind at the time of recording. Particular favourite topics include creativity and all the arts — music, films, screenplays, fiction, poetry, comics, games, comedy, and everything in between. Messages from listeners welcomed for possible inclusion in an episode. Note that sending a recording for inclusion in an episode of this podcast does indeed implicitly give me permission to do so.

What is this?

It is a transcript of every episode from the 1st season of my first podcast series, *What Now with Simo*.

I would have named it just *What Now*, but that was already in use, many times over, plus it would have been hopeless in terms of searchability.

There are some benefits to having a name described by one friend as Lovecraftian. Even one fragment of that name makes for instantly improved findability.[1]

* * *

Editorially there were two choices for this book: faithful transcription or wholesale re-editing into something like essays.

For numerous reasons I by far prefer the first option. This is another form of presenting the same material, and I did want to present the *same* material.

I also find the resulting texts more interesting in this unedited form. There are also questions of information density and memorability that make me sure this was the best decision.[2]

---

[1] Unfortunately I'm not the only one with these three names ever to have lived. This fact is the bane of my visibility on Google. There was at least one other person with this name who lived before my time and — curses — also happened to be an artist. My nemesis. The very sight of — just kidding.

[2] Many books — like some textbooks written for students — fail to present the material memorably for the reason that every sentence in them is meant to be remembered. They would achieve their aim better if there were an ebb and flow of denser and looser passages. Likewise, something being a little skewed

Plus this way all the content becomes available for anyone with any hearing loss.

* * *

For grammar and punctuation hawks:

As happens with spoken language, there are moments of creative grammar here. Mistakes, some call them. All those were knowingly left in.

Likewise I adopt a relaxed and flexible attitude towards commas. Every comma and absence of one is intentional. Languages are living, creative things.

When writing, editing, proofreading, or translating something for someone else, I'll produce 100% accurate and grammatical English, as sophisticated as desired. And since I may also in the future wish to write something for someone else, the direction in which I've consciously taken my use of language in my private life and for my own projects might be seen as shooting myself in the foot.

---

or unusual is immediately more memorable. Many poets and songwriters have an instinctive or conscious understanding of this.

The fact remains that as a private person and for the purposes of my creative work I now prefer to use English that doesn't stray too near to the Queen's English.

Poetry, the First Nations short stories of W. P. Kinsella,[3] David Lynch, and many other influences have shown me there are more expressive and meaningful forms of English than that. So these days I aim for something in that direction.

* * *

Most of the people in this world don't speak perfect English. Many haven't had the opportunities in life for schooling like that, and many have dyslexia. That is no reason to look down on or make fun of them.

So no, I have no sympathy for language Nazis. It's a selfish and entitled attitude to take, especially in this day and age, when everyone should know better.

* * *

---

[3] The first two collections of these are *Dance Me Outside* (1977) and *Scars* (1978).

I'm also really interested in the evolution of non-fiction as well as fiction books. Among my favourite books and inspirations for this and future works have been John Cage's *Silence: Lectures and Writings by John Cage* (1961) and David Lynch's *Catching the Big Fish: Meditation, Consciousness, and Creativity* (2006). Both blew away the assumptions I had subconsciously had about the limits of what books can be.

I was also thrilled when I flipped through one of Kim Stanley Robinson's science fiction novels in a bookstore and saw that he had whole chapters that were just lists — listing landscape features or things seen, or something of that nature. (I have read his works intermittently in chronological order and haven't yet gotten to that novel, so I'm vague on this point.)

And I enjoy reading materials that were originally spoken. Interviews, transcribed talks, dictated memoirs, and such. Rod Serling wrote by speaking into a recorder.[4] David Lynch often writes by speaking. Reading text produced

---

[4] A Dictaphone.

this way is a whole different thing than reading something created all along as text on a page.

There's a biography of J. D. Salinger called *Salinger* (2014) by David Shields and Shane Salerno. It's an oral biography made up of segments of interview materials, quote after quote, with each person telling things in their own words. A collage of quotes. Again, spoken words on a page.

Books can be anything.

* * *

I'm interested in the relationship between spoken and written language. How something written sounds when spoken aloud and how something spoken aloud reads when written down.

Spoken language moves through time and appears to us one word at a time, whereas the written word we can see in diagram, from a height, the layout of it, as it lies on the page, and our eye can go sometimes in less than a blink of an eye from one part of the text to another.

A thread of thought may seem to be leading somewhere,

particularly when being spoken, and on the written page it can be seen to be a side path that is only seen so far until it disappears behind the trees — like one of the "that's another story to be told another time" crossroads in Michael Ende's *The Neverending Story* (1979). I see value in such meandering.

Sometimes meandering down little byways that peter out — or seeing others do so — can lead to things more useful than fully completed roads or thoughts.

* * *

Many thanks to everyone who has listened to the podcast or is reading this book, and extra special thanks to Maren for her great message for episode 1.7 and for her permission to include it in this printed edition.

Wishing you a great day and good reading.

—Simo Sakari Aaltonen, Tampere, 24th of May 2020

1.1 Corona, Krónur, and Creativity

Greetings, and welcome to the first episode of my podcast, which I am calling *What Now with Simo*.

To open this up by explaining the title, it simply refers to the fact that I want this to be a spontaneous and unplanned podcast. And actually I'm thinking of it more as like a late-night radio programme might be. Something that you can listen to that isn't like a high-pressure, hard-sell kind of thing.

And I am not going to do much in terms of fancy tricks, and I'm going to start out very minimal and see how I want to evolve this over time. But it's important for me not to make this a thing that I would stop enjoying doing. So I am keeping things simple for now.

I would say that your enjoyment of this podcast will depend largely on whether you find my way of expressing myself and my way of thinking something that you enjoy or not. If not, then I would recommend simply of course finding the things in this world that you really do enjoy.

Life is too short.

I encourage everyone to only follow those things that really speak to you. That's one thing I want to say right off. I'm not going to try to make this something that will keep everyone's attention. I'm not going to think in terms of how many minutes I've been talking about something. I may talk about the same thing for a long time or just jump from one topic to another. That's actually how my thought processes work.

It is also pretty much how I see life working, when we really look at it. It's usually not only a linear progression from place A to B. There are surprises, sudden shifts, of all kinds, on every level, and so I think this is more how life works. And I think it's boring to have something that is planned always and that always proceeds according to some layout or script and so on.

You may also notice a lot of experimentation as I make these first episodes in particular. I'm going to see what kind of results I'm most happy with in terms of how far I am from the microphone. My thinking on this may not be

the same as people usually have, which seems to be —
people these days favour very close microphone
placement, which can sometimes give the feeling that the
person is talking straight into your ear.

This would lead me easily into another fascinating topic —
fascinating to me, at least — which goes back all the way to
the early days of recording and recorded music. But let's
leave that for another time, because I want to keep this first
episode fairly short and focus for now on what I want this
to be.

And I mentioned that *What Now* is like a descriptive title,
in that it is what is happening now: what I'm thinking
about, the things foremost on my mind, anything that is
interesting me at that moment. And I will also occasionally
speak some about my own life, but only when it relates to
some topic.

Or I should say most of the time when it relates to some
topic. Sometimes I may mention something just because I
feel like it. Again, I'm very keen to avoid setting any
boundaries to this.

That is also why the title is so abstract. It can cover anything, because the "what" can be anything and, well, the moment it happens is now. So, yeah, that's pretty much the title.

And I'm also going to describe my situation when it comes to the coronavirus — COVID-19 — situation. I'm recording this from Iceland, from a hotel where I am staying. I started my trip here just before they started strongly advising against travel.

At the point when I left on my trip, which I had planned a long time in advance, I took careful measure of the situation and looked into it and did the research, and looked at the recommendations of the Finnish official pages of the foreign ministry and the Icelandic recommendations also. Iceland has even their own COVID-19 info pages. And none of those recommended against travel at that point. But that changed shortly after my arrival.

So I have, for the safety of everyone — not only myself, of course — I have mostly stayed in my hotel room and doing my work, and creative work also. And I will be talking about both of those over the course of this podcast series.

I still don't feel comfortable calling it a podcast, because that sets certain expectations in people's minds. And I am almost going to be like an anti-podcast podcast. Because I don't want to do any of the things that I noticed I had subconsciously absorbed as being something that I *assumed* everyone expects from a podcast. I want this to be, like I said, a relaxed thing, a calming thing.

And this is also my attempt to start leaving a more lasting and meaningful legacy than I have been able to do for example via social media. I have noticed over the years that social media are not the right places — I'm using the plural because "media" is plural — it's not the right place for many of the things that I most want to talk about.

And anyway, most of the things you put on social media — they just sink after posting. They shortly afterwards just disappear. So it's not a way to create a legacy.

* * *

I think there is something very unique about hearing a person's thoughts and feelings expressed in their own voice.

I have the greatest respect for writing. And of course I myself am a writer also. But I have to say that I'm very grateful for the recorded works — I should say, I'm calling them actually works — but I'm referring to, like, interviews and appearances that were recorded by some of my favourite creative people, like Ray Bradbury. He did tons of interviews in his lifetime. He happens to be one of my favourite writers, by the way, and I will most likely mention him quite often in episodes to come.

On the other hand, there are some people, of course, who I admire greatly and of whom we have either no or very few voice samples of. And I find that it really helps to form a connection and to get the nuances of their thought and them as people when you can hear their voice. I think it's a wonderful thing, and really I think we should be grateful, to be able to do this.

I don't mean only to make, for example, podcasts. I'm

talking of the very act of speaking. We actually can express ourselves in this magical way. I'm not exaggerating, I think, in saying it that way.

The likelihood is that many people will not like this podcast at all. Many will hate my voice. Some may like it. Some may be indifferent. But, in the end, I believe that the only thing we really have that we can offer to the world is ourselves. There is no point in trying to do something that somebody else can do, or be the same way that somebody else is. Because that already exists. You don't need to duplicate it.

That's why to me it can be frustrating when people who are very unique and whom I admire very much sometimes compare themselves to some famous person and say that they wish they were more like that famous person in this or that aspect. Because the reality is that what makes that person[5] so beautiful is the unique combination of all the things that they are — and are *not*. I'm talking both

---

[5] The one comparing herself or himself with someone else and feeling unhappy about it.

externally and internally: how they look, but of course more importantly how they are deep down. The combination of everything that they are. That is, in the end, the most precious thing that you can share.

And I find that the creative people whom I admire the most are the ones who have found ways to give of themselves and to give permission to themselves to be, deeply, just themselves. Not in a selfish way. But to let the best of themselves develop and grow.

As you can see, I can express a simple thought in many, many words. In this case I just wanted to say that this is my way of trying to put myself out there in such a way that if it works for someone, then it works. If my voice is comforting to someone, then I am very glad. If it feels like anything positive in this difficult time, or in times to come... You know, there will be a time when I will be gone, one day. It might be many decades from now, or sooner. Because we really never can know. And I think that's a healthy thing to keep in mind.

But anyway, there will come a time when I am gone and

what will remain behind are the things I created and the memories I left behind. And this podcast, I think, will be worth more than any amount of text-only social media posts or memes that I might share.

I have to believe that there are people who can relate to something I'm doing, or the way I am as a person. Otherwise I wouldn't be doing this. After all, that's something that every creative person — when they put themselves out there, it does involve implicitly the feeling that what they are doing is worth it. Because it means something to *them*. And because we are all, you know, part of this same huge thing called life, it can mean something for others as well.

And I have actually struggled over the years to be really myself in the way I express myself, because I used to try to be more logical and express myself in ways that actually didn't really reflect the way I think or the way I am.

This rambling, long introduction may give you some idea of how I actually work and how I actually am as a person.

* * *

I just don't think that any of us have time to waste in this
life.

I have tried over the years to open up as much as I can —
without being stupid about it. There are people who want
to harm other people, of course. But as much as I can open
myself up, creatively, and to speak from the heart — those
are things that really matter to me. And this podcast is my
maybe biggest step so far.

I really had many, many years in my life, up until recently,
when I really just hated hearing my own voice. But it
happened over the last several years — or I should say
maybe even a decade — that there were various
friendships — but I should say actually only a handful of
friendships — I could even go further and say that I'm
talking mainly of a few people — with whom I was able to
start having a regular exchange by words. Whether it was
by Skype or Messenger voice or video calls or WhatsApp
or in real life. And I think I got better, slowly, over that
time, in expressing myself. And I noticed when sometimes

I would listen back to some of these messages I was leaving, when I was talking to a friend and we were sharing some of our thoughts — I realised that I no longer disliked my own way of expressing myself so much.

That doesn't mean that I think I'm so great. It doesn't mean that I'm special, except the same way that everyone is. But it means that I feel ready to do this.

People who have been in contact with me on social media may have noticed that I have really not shared almost anything where I speak. Except two things that I can think of. No, well, three things. But those were just social media things that I had up for a while. Some of them actually are still available. Maybe even all — all three that I'm thinking of.

But all the rest I did in silence.

Like, I recorded myself playing piano very badly several years ago when I was just practising. I had started to teach myself music. And I didn't speak in them because at that point I didn't know how to do it in such a way that I could feel that I'm expressing myself in a way I can be happy with.

* * *

I guess an important part of the first episode is to say a few words about the logo I have chosen. It is a key ring in which there are the two most familiar musical clefs. They're called clefs. The word comes from old French — the word "clef". And it actually just meant "key" — like a key to a door. The word has changed in modern French, and I believe it's *clé* or something like that.

What you see on the key ring are the treble clef and the bass clef. And of course the most common contexts in which people see these are on the piano grand staff. The treble is for the higher part, the bass obviously for the lower part. Even though these are musical symbols, to me this symbol of these things together, the ring and — you know, because a ring is a circle. A circle represents completion and completeness. By having this symbol I am trying to encapsulate — for myself if no one else, it's not really important whether the symbol is understood — I'm trying to say that this podcast will cover everything from the highest to the lowest, and far and wide.

Or I should say not necessarily that it *will* cover. But there are no limits to it. I didn't want to start a podcast only about music, for example, as maybe suggested by this symbol.

I will talk a lot about music because music is something that has always been very important to me, and in recent years I started studying it really seriously in order to be able to create some myself. I have ended up becoming a composer, and I am actually now working on my first large-scale composition, which I am going to publish later this year, and it is called *An Iceland Symphony*.

* * *

The name comes from not only the fact that I wrote a lot of the music for that in 2019 — the first few months of 2019, when I was in Iceland just by myself, meeting no one in that period of time. I was doing a lot of creating in that time. And also because it reflects many of my feelings, things that have either happened or that have some meaning to me — it all kind of went into the music naturally. And it's also an Iceland symphony because it is something that happened in Iceland.

(It's not _The Iceland Symphony_. It would be crazy to call any symphony that. At least if the person were being serious.)

And while I've been here now only for a short while this time — this is my fourth visit to Iceland as I record this — I continued working on that symphony, piecing it still together. It needs finalising and putting the pieces together, and so on.

And I'm creating demo versions of different parts of it. Hopefully in the end I'll have reasonably representative demo versions of the whole work that I can play or share with someone who might be interested in actually performing or publishing this.

I am going to start looking for a music publisher also at the same time, but most likely I will self-publish this.

* * *

And so to sum up that symbol, to me that's the most concise encapsulation of anything and everything. It goes from the highest note to the lowest note.

I should also mention, in case somebody listens to this podcast sometime far in the future, and if in fact it did happen — and by "it" I mean that there is the possibility that I will at some point decide that I want to change the title of my podcast — and why not? After all, it's my thing, and there's no rule about it. If I think of a title that would leave me the same kind of freedom, then I would choose it. But for now, I thought it was time to get started with this and not go for perfection.

I think perfection — ideas of everything needing to be just right, or giving up — that's a problem for many creative people. Or if not giving up, then stalling forever, which can be a slower form of giving up. Because one day the days will be over, the nights will be over, and if you haven't done it by then, it will never happen.

* * *

I should mention what my situation is with regard to my return to Finland. Because at this point all Finnish citizens who have their permanent residence in Finland have been advised to return back to Finland, and I have been waiting around for several days to see what will happen, because my flight company, the airline that I am using, has been drowned under by contact attempts, of course, from people all over the world trying to make their own arrangements.

And I already had a ticket, a return ticket back to Finland, reserved for the 31st of this month — the last of this month. But that flight, I learned only today, has been cancelled, and I was able to get an earlier flight.

Without giving too much details about my travel plans — broadcasting it to the whole world, who must be listening, of course — I will only say that I will be leaving in some days after recording this. I still have some time here in Iceland.

So I will continue here until my trip, doing my own things and working on my Iceland symphony. And I must say that I think this trip also added something to that symphony that would not have been there if I had not made this trip.

I often make choices intuitively, and they may not seem like they are practically justified. To make a trip that has no specific purpose other than to be working and creating, mostly at a hotel room, and not even meeting other people — to some people that might sound a bit crazy. We all have our own things that help us in life. For me, travel and a change of scenery are often very important for that.

And to me, Iceland is a very special and unique country. If I had never experienced Iceland and had the fortune to know some Icelanders, I would never have created this symphony, for example. And it would never be — any music I would have made would not have been — the way it's going to be.

While aiming to pretty much wrap this first episode up now, I should say how much I have appreciated all my contacts with Iceland and Icelanders. People here have been — the majority of them have been — wonderful. And the good experiences have far outweighed any negative ones.

* * *

Right now, by the way — this is one thing I also wanted to mention about this podcast — you may hear some ambient sounds. There is traffic outside the window. I'm not going to eliminate any environmental sounds. I will be, in the future, recording this in many different places, just wherever I happen to be.

This is one of those things that I referred to earlier. For some strange reason I had absorbed this clinical thinking about making a podcast, that things would have to be pristine and hi-fi, and I would have to get everything technically right.

Then I asked myself: "Why do I assume any of this, and why am I setting these limits on myself?"

For example, are environmental sounds not a wonderful thing? Why would you want to eliminate that? Why would you want to do only something very studio-bound? Unless you happen to be in a city and doing like a radio interview programme and you actually have to isolate a lot of the sound.

But if the sounds you're hearing is traffic in the

background or the sound of rain on windowpanes, then those only add to the experience, as far as I'm concerned.

I remember I was once making one of these very brief videos where I just sat on a piano stool I had at that time — I had a white digital piano at that time — and when I made the recording, I just recorded with a microphone that was off to one side, and when I sat down, the chair creaked.

And I noticed that even if I were watching this as something created by somebody else, I would have liked that detail of the chair creaking.

I don't like how clinical and overprocessed things have become in many fields of art and entertainment. That's not really life anymore, or lifelike.

I like to have some texture, and I like watching and listening to things in any kind of quality as long as the content is worth it. I watch a lot of YouTube videos where it's below VHS video quality. Or, talking of another field, I listen to a lot of old music. A lot of it, of course, is very limited in the range of reproduction they were capable of then. And in my own case, for example, I prefer to listen to the recordings from those old days that have kept the crackle. If you eliminate the crackle, you also eliminate part of the music, and it starts sounding like something muffled inside, like, some kind of fabric container. That is actually just very poor remastering if they lose so much of the music.

Anyway, I like record crackle. I like the crackle of fireplaces. My dream home in the future — which would be like a warm house on a hill — it would have a fireplace, of course.

* * *

So I think this is a good place to start wrapping up this first episode. I want to say just a few more words.

I want to tell people that the world situation with the coronavirus — this is something that we just need to get through. And the way to get through it is simply to make the clever choices, to remain calm, and help each other out.

If you have people that you are not sure are okay, why not reach out to them and ask them: "How are you doing? Are

you okay?" Whether they are young people, old people —
just anyone that you can think of that you know. Make sure
that they're okay. That's very important.

I have some experience of loneliness and isolation and
things like that, and maybe I'll talk some more about that
in the future, though not in a depressing way — that is
something I'm determined on: not to be depressing — but
as just experiences I've been through.

You will notice I'm saying "I have been through", which
means that they were survivable — in the end.

To many people this isolation has come as a shock, and
they have difficulty adjusting to it, and it is frightening. To
me it has not been so frightening because I have had many
experiences in life that have in a way, I would say,
prepared me to be better able to cope with this now. So
there is a silver lining to even unpleasant and painful life
experiences.

Again, I just want to say that if you are feeling anxious
about all this, just know that this is a time that will pass.

One day we will go to concerts again, we can be in the open air, we can run up to our friend that we've missed and hug them tight.

All that is going to happen in the future. For now we just need to sit tight. This may be a good time to reflect on those things that we have been doing in our lives that may not have been the right way to live this life. I am also speaking to myself at the same time and reminding myself about how important it is not to get drawn down by petty things, or bitterness.

You know, it's okay to feel bitter if things have happened that have been painful. It's okay to feel bitterness. I don't like the kind of thinking that says you have to always be positive and only smile and pretend like everything's okay. No. You just need to be honest. And work towards getting past the bitterness, for example, in this case, if we are talking of just this one emotion. But the same thing applies to anything else.

Even though, of course, nobody wished for this to happen — it is going to cause and already has caused great suffering, great pain, loss of life, and we don't yet know how bad it will be — it's going to be over one day. I just want to encourage everyone who may be feeling downhearted and even maybe a little bit beaten by this thing. It's only a temporary thing. We will have the world again. It will be something that we can't yet know exactly what it's going to be like. It may be a whole new kind of world. But, it will have a lot of the old beautiful things in it. And maybe some new beautiful things as well.

I would say that almost certainly a lot of us will be very, very glad when we can again do the things that maybe — because we had gotten so used to them — we had started to take for granted. That's just human nature and psychology that a little bit of that happens to everyone. Or a lot of it. Again, it's okay. You don't have to feel bad about it.

But, you know, this is how we grow as people. We recognise that there is something that we have not been able to enjoy, and sometimes it just takes that distance. You have to be away from something — or, indeed, someone —

to know their real value to you. Being unable to hug...

In my case, I will be unable to even go see my parents when I return to Finland, for at least 14 days. After that it is apparently allowed for family members to see each other, even if they are in a risk group.

* * *

I'm thinking of all my friends and all the people I care about. Whether I'm in contact with them or not, I will just say that I hope you are all doing well, and I hope that you will stay safe through this.

Make the smart choices. And help the people around you and the people that you know make the smart choices as well. We will get through this together.

* * *

I want to finish this first podcast by reading a Shakespeare sonnet that I happened to come across while reading an issue of a magazine from the time of the Second World War.

* * *

From you have I been absent in the spring,

When proud-pied April dressed in all his trim

Hath put a spirit of youth in everything,

That heavy Saturn laughed and leaped with him.

Yet nor the lays of birds nor the sweet smell

Of different flowers in odour and in hue

Could make me any summer's story tell,

Or from their proud lap pluck them where they grew.

Nor did I wonder at the lily's white,

Nor praise the deep vermilion in the rose.

They were but sweet, but figures of delight,

Drawn after you, you pattern of all those.

    Yet seemed it winter still and, you away,

    As with your shadow I with these did play.

* * *

Good night, and thank you for listening.

1.2 Last Flight for Now, Comedy, and All Summer in a Day

Greetings, and welcome to the second episode of my podcast series.

I thought I'd explain to anyone who listened to the first episode or saw its title that the word *krónur* in that title, which was "Corona, *Krónur*, and Creativity" — *krónur* is the plural of *króna*, which is the Icelandic currency. So it was simply a reference to my being in Iceland.

Speaking of which, my time in Iceland is now growing short. This is actually my last day in Iceland for the foreseeable future, and it is quite sad to be thinking that there is no telling when I'll have this pleasure again.

I'm of course on the other hand grateful that I got to make this last trip before having to then stay in Finland for the foreseeable future. And of course I'll be starting my 14-day quarantine when I get back.

It's a rainy day here, with strong winds. Some slushy snow

or rain. Mostly water, I think. And I just left to go to the store.

They are now taking stronger measures also here. At this store I go to that is nearest to the hotel I am staying at, they are now limiting the number of people allowed at one time in the store to 60, and for a while already there has been a notification. And it's actually recommended for anywhere in the country, as I understand. But in the store there is a special notice about it that you should stay at least two metres distant from other people.

* * *

This second episode will be quite brief because I have a lot to do — travel preparations to take care of. I thought I'd use this brief time to make some recommendations.

But before that I wanted to mention something amusing that made me smile. The local police department here in the southwest of Iceland — they issued a notice a few days ago asking criminals to kindly cancel their plans. This was reported by the *Iceland Monitor*, a website in English. Their notice went like this:

> "Due to the situation created by COVID-19, or the
> coronavirus, as it's called, the police kindly ask those who
> have been contemplating breaking the law to cancel all such
> plans until further notice."

So that's the notice from the police department in this part
of Iceland.

* * *

I was surprised to learn that Dame Vera Lynn — apologies
if I'm mispronouncing the name, it might be "Veh-ra"
Lynn... "Vee-ra" Lynn... I'm not sure which one — Vera
Lynn, who I thought might have well passed on already,
and I had assumed so — she is actually still alive. She's
now one hundred and three years old.

And if you don't recognise the name, she was a singer that
played an important role in the Second World War in terms
of motivating the troops. She became famous especially for
the song "We'll Meet Again". Her rendering of that song
was an inspiration in a time that was even more difficult

than what we are going through now.

That reminds me that I do want to make the point that even though we are going through difficult times now, we may find some perspective in thinking about what the people who went through World War II had to face. For example that, and many other things in history, but if we consider just World War II, it meant people forced to leave their loved ones behind and to go kill or be killed, or maim or be maimed, or any combination of those. To be traumatised, to be tortured, or any number of inhumane things.

Compared to that, having to stay home and to take precautions about hygiene is not exactly the worst fate in the world. Yes, it is sad and it is difficult, and there are people dying. But people not so far removed from our time, and some of them of course still alive, went through far greater difficulties, more painful experiences than most of us will face during this epidemic. I think that's worth bearing in mind.

This is also one of the things that makes it important to be aware of history: to have some perspective on our hardships, and on the other hand regarding all the ways we are very lucky.

And now the very thing that many people have deplored, which is all our devices — we are probably all very grateful for them now. Imagine how much more out of touch we would be if we'd be just writing letters to each other.

I've never myself been one of the people who said that these devices as such are somehow making us more antisocial or dehumanising us. They are not. And for many, they have all along been ways to keep better in contact with other people. And now, of course, they are vital. Like the internet and the social media are.

This may give us some perspective on how bad or good these things are. I say they are almost only good. By far the good outweighs the bad.

* * *

And now I think I need to already start wrapping up this

episode. It was a very brief one.

But this is one of the things that I like about doing my podcast in such a freeform way. I don't have to make the episodes of uniform length, because there's no one telling me I have to. So I won't. Some will be short, some will be long, some will be somewhere in between.

But before I go, I wanted to make those recommendations I referred to earlier.

* * *

I think comedy is very important. And especially when it comes to painful times.

Comedy can go too far. It can be mean. But of course I'm not talking about that kind of comedy. I don't like comedians who are just spreading their mean-spirited selves around.

To me, a comedian who I'm really grateful to have discovered — which I only did in the early part of 2019, when I was just by myself in Iceland — is the Canadian stand-up comic Norm Macdonald.

In that time I started watching videos featuring him on YouTube — his performances and appearances on talk shows and in interviews. And I warmly recommend him if you are looking for something new in this area. He is one of the very few comedians who actually makes me laugh. Like actually *makes* me laugh. Not only makes me *want* to laugh. And not only that, he also makes me smile.[6]

A lot of his humour dances on the edge and sometimes steps over the edge of what might be called "good taste" by some people. But having seen enough from him, I know that he has a really good heart, and when he makes jokes about painful subjects, sometimes in ways that are quite outrageous, he has the best motive in mind. He is in fact doing something that is relieving a painful tension that people may have about that subject.[7]

_____

[6] Here I was paraphrasing something he himself said in an episode of *Norm Macdonald Live*.

[7] Instead of saying this is his motive — this misses the thought I was trying to express — I should have said this is the effect his comedy has. If it were an active, conscious motive, the result probably wouldn't be funny. So I misspoke here.

I will definitely be talking more about him in the future, but for now, if you don't recognise the name Norm Macdonald, then I would warmly recommend, for example, looking up his last — for now — stand-up appearance, where he does stand-up about the coronavirus. Many comedians might do that in a cynical, exploitative way, but he is not one of them. I can recommend going on YouTube, finding "Norm Macdonald does stand-up about the coronavirus", or something similar. I'm sure you'll find it.

It's actually in two parts. And they are only part of this stand-up appearance. Somebody was taking the video, I think surreptitiously — I think it wasn't like an official recording — but he himself has shared that, so he's okay with it. To me, the material is gold and his delivery is always gold. He is really a very natural comedian.

One reason I really love him is that he has this relaxed way of presenting himself and talking. Many comedians make me feel exhausted after just a few minutes, if not less, after listening to them.

But with Norm Macdonald, I could listen to him, and I have listened to him, for hours on end sometimes. I used to listen to his interviews and talk show appearances and all the other things from him on YouTube while falling asleep, starting early last year.

Another thing I really like about him is that he's not trying too hard. He doesn't care whether he gets a laugh or not. When I say he doesn't care, I mean that in the best sense. Because he enjoys people's reactions even if it is no laughter for some joke. That can sometimes seem to amuse him even more than getting a laugh.

So he's not taking himself too seriously or stressing out about it, like many comedians are.

* * *

The other recommendation I would like to make, now that most of us are having to stay in isolation — it is a very beautiful story written by Ray Bradbury as a short story, but the version I'm recommending of that story is a TV adaptation from the 1980s.

It is available on YouTube, and you will find it in its entirety by searching with the words "Ray Bradbury" and the title of the story, "All Summer in a Day".

"All Summer in a Day".

And that is a perfect title for that story. It's a story that is extremely poignant, and in this time in particular, I think people will be even more able to relate to it. It is one of those stories that if it doesn't move you, if it doesn't make you feel something, then there might be something wrong.

I don't want to "sell" anything I recommend too hard. I don't like that kind of approach when I'm listening to someone else talk about something. But I feel sure that if you take the time to watch this adaptation — I would recommend watching it in the evening, with your loved ones (if you are fortunate enough to have any) with you — it is less than half an hour — I believe that you will be very glad that you watched it.

It's the kind of thing that it's now difficult to imagine even being made, because everything is now so processed and artificial in many ways. This is simply a group of very fine actors — including very fine young actors — and real locations. No CGI.

And actually this TV version, this adaptation, even improves on the original short story that Ray Bradbury wrote. It's that good — that the ending is even more beautiful and moving to me in this adaptation.

The only thing I will add — that it is a story told from the perspective of a young girl. The people in the story — for a different reason — are living an isolated experience.

It's one of those stories where, after it's over, at least I myself get a clear feeling of perspective. Remembering what are the important things in life.

* * *

Now I have to get going. I want to thank you for listening, and good night.

1.3 Back Here, David Lynch, and the Dalai Lama

Greetings, and welcome to the third episode of my podcast.

It just occurred to me that I have never yet said my full name in any of these. I'm not fussy about how anyone pronounces my name. You can call me anything you like. As long as you don't call me for dinner. For now — for the time being.

Once this thing with the thing is over, then I would like to be called for dinner. But for now, if for some strange reason you had to be having dinner with someone and somebody said, "Pass the salt," the right response would be, "Pass."

My name is Simo Sakari Aaltonen. Finnish doesn't aspirate. It's not "tuh" in, for example, "Aal-to-nen". It's "Aaltonen". We say it softer.

But I actually like even more the way some people from other countries have pronounced my name. Like somebody I know said it "Simoh", and I came to prefer that, even though it's not the Finnish pronunciation.

So, please, when one day some of us will have the fortune to be meeting face to face or talking over the internet, on a call or something, then there is no reason to worry about this.

* * *

Today has been Day 1 of my 14-day quarantine, which is now required because I came back to Finland from another country. And yesterday I got up at 6 a.m., and I was home only a little bit past 2 a.m. the next night.

I flew from the Icelandic international airport in Keflavík to Heathrow in London. That plane was not so full.

Then I needed to wait for two hours at Heathrow, which was not bad at all. Finnair was very nice in the arrangements they made for me to reschedule and plan this new flight, free of charge. So I didn't even have to pay for the changes to my original return flight.

After two hours at Heathrow I flew to Helsinki, and that

plane arrived at almost 11 in the evening. And then I still needed to travel to my apartment in Tampere. T-A-M-P-E-R-E.

Of course in some of the places on that journey there were people near me, and the plane to Helsinki was quite full. So there were people right next to me then. But not anyone visibly or audibly ill. But of course one can be a carrier without symptoms.

But of course I took all precautions. I have always had hand sanitiser with me while travelling abroad, even before this situation arose. And that was actually the only reason I had it with me now. Because people had started hoarding it, so the pharmacies in Finland were out of hand sanitiser at that point.

When I left Iceland, I had noticed that some places had started manufacturing their own hand sanitiser. And in the grocery store I went to there, they had a whole pallet full of bottles of that. People are catching up with this situation and creating ways to cope with it.

Like I said, there of course was exposure to other people on the way. That was unavoidable. But I also really had no choice except to take this flight now, because Finland had instructed all Finnish citizens with a permanent residence in Finland to return now. And in this situation, I guess it was the only sensible choice. Also considering other things.

I want to thank everyone who has reached out to me in this time and asked me how I am doing. People who have shown caring.

Today I was again, of course, checking out information about the coronavirus situation, and I noticed that I need to pull back from reading about it a little bit now, especially because I'm in my 14-day quarantine.

The reality is that it is a very serious thing. It is way more dangerous than ordinary flu.

But also, like I just said to my father when I spoke to him on the phone, one day this will be over. It's not going to be like this forever. It may feel like that for now. But the world is going to open again one day, and we'll be able to do all the things that we are now missing.

There are also some positive things that can come out of this. Certainly I think people will be able to appreciate more the things we can't be doing now. And the people we can't be seeing in person, now.

I didn't read the article, but I saw a headline today where a psychologist said that we are now missing one basic human thing. Which is the ability to hug.

Won't it be nice when one day we will be able to shake hands also, without worry?

I saw at least two friends of mine say the same thing on social media the other day, so I don't know if one of them heard it from the other or not, or if this is already like a meme, but the gist of it was to ask:

Will those of us who survive this come out of this as agoraphobic alcoholics?

Speaking of which, I would recommend avoiding drinking in this time, and especially if you are ill. Alcohol does lower your immunological capacity, so your body would be less able to fight off disease.

And of course that's true anyway, even outside of this special health crisis we're having now.

But also, I wanted to mention another thing. I'm not sure if I'm saying something that is known by almost everybody already, but it has been studied well and established that stress and fear — these primal responses — they lower your immunological capacity for the time that you are feeling them.

And I guess probably for some time after, since it takes your body time to recover.

There was one study in particular that I remember where they monitored the immunological response of people watching the opening minutes of *Saving Private Ryan*. I have actually not seen that movie, but I gather that it starts with a big fight sequence.[8]

It was described by, I believe, one of my English professors at the University of Jyväskylä in Finland, a long time ago now —

---

[8] You can say that again. It's only the Battle of Normandy.

(His name is Michael Coleman, and I hope he is alive and well. He was one of my favourite professors, a really genial, likeable Irish guy.)

— he described the opening by saying something like, "If you watch that, you start to ask yourself, 'Will I get out of this situation alive?'"

At least I remember it being Professor Coleman who said that. Sorry if I have misattributed this quote. But I'm again getting lost from my main point.

The point I was referring to that movie was that the study showed that during those opening minutes, the immunological capacity of the people watching it significantly lowered.

Which means that in those moments they were more susceptible, more likely to catch something. Or if their body was already fighting something, then the bodies in question — that sounds like the title of a murder mystery, if it's not already — but the bodies in question would be less able to fight anything that they may already have been dealing with.

To me this is an interesting question for many reasons. And one of them is, of course, that we can study scientifically the effects of art and entertainment on the human body. In some matters, at least.

I do wish that that study had also followed what happens later, when the subjects watched that movie. But I believe the finding was only about those opening minutes. I would like to know, did later events in the film somehow mitigate that effect?

Not that I know about the later events, because as I mentioned, I haven't seen the film. And you can be sure I'm not going to watch it *now*. I have no wish to have my immunological response lowered right now in particular. But like I said, this is an interesting question.

I find that this is a topic — whenever I have tried to bring it up as a matter of discussion, on social media, for example, people have strange objections to the idea of art and entertainment actually having effects on us.

Which, to me, is very strange. Because of course nothing can be experienced without it having effects on you. Because it's the same thing. The experience *is* an experience because you are having reactions to something. Nothing can go through your mind or your feelings without that affecting the stuff happening in your body and brain.

And one reason I wonder about the turn that a lot of entertainment has taken these days, which has been to hammer harder at the viewer with ever more graphic violence and so on…

I want to make it clear that I'm not against violence in entertainment or art. I'm very much against it in real life, unless needed for self-defence. If somebody attacked a friend of mine, I would do anything it took to stop that attack.

I love David Lynch's movies, which often have very extreme violence in them, including some scenes that, when I was younger and was experiencing them — they were quite capable of creating extreme anxiety. More than any other director that I know of.

But he also knows how to do the other end. The light. And he's unique in that sense, in my experience, among directors on that level. That he can do both the extremest darkness but also the extremest light, and everything in between.

And he has the best sense of humour out of anyone with that kind of range and doing often dark work. David Lynch is, of course, completely unique in any sense. He has such an amazing sense of humour. I have laughed as hard with some of his work as with anything else in my life.

And I remember that was the thing that really clinched my love for him, in addition to the wonderful darkness and the wonderful light — but also the fact that he could really make me burst out laughing.

It's not necessarily well known — yet — but it was mentioned in his co-written biography *Room to Dream* —

(Which I highly recommend and which is also available on Spotify, for example, as a complete audiobook version, and it includes parts that are not in the book. So to get the fullest experience of *Room to Dream*, I would recommend both the book and the audiobook. The book alternates chapters written by his co-author, Kristine McKenna, in the third person — she relates the backgrounds and the chronological events — and then after each of those chapters there's a chapter by David Lynch himself, speaking directly of his memories and adding details and comments.)

— but what I was going to mention from that book is that when Mr. Lynch was younger, he read *MAD* magazine. He read it with his friends, and they would laugh their head off. So that magazine played a role in forming his sense of humour. Which I can't tell you how much I admire that quality in him. That tells me that he's the real deal.

I think it can be worrying if somebody doesn't have a sense of humour, at all. Including a sense of humour about themselves. That's very important, of course. It's also a worrying thing if somebody only has a sense of humour about others.

David Lynch is the real deal, just like the Dalai Lama is the real deal. He genuinely believes the things he says and does. I don't know how many people realise it — how funny the Dalai Lama can be.

* * *

I saw him in person many years ago when he visited Finland. He's visited Finland several times. I forget how many. I went to Helsinki to see him. I'm very glad I can say that I have seen the Dalai Lama live.

Before that I had listened to many interviews with him, and I had come to admire his way of expressing himself. His English is wonderful.

It's poetic and descriptive in a way that I find with some people from other countries in particular for whom English is not their first language. I genuinely mean it that I think that kind of English can be even more expressive and even lyrical — it has a poetic quality — than the English of native speakers of that language.

One of my favourite examples of the Dalai Lama's sense of

humour is the story he told in one of his books, I think — I haven't read many books by or about him, but in one of them he mentioned that even though as a Tibetan Buddhist monk he's not supposed to eat anything after midnight and before morning, he still sometimes sneaks out to get some cookies.

And of course he has a very genuine, authentic laugh as well. I think he can be very funny. And again, to me that's a very healthy sign in a spiritual leader.

And I think it's a good way to identify people who shouldn't really be trusted much. What I mean is, if somebody lacks a sense of humour, that's a real warning sign.

Johnny Depp said in some interview in *Death Ray* magazine — there was a magazine called *Death Ray* published in the UK for a short time several years ago — and in that interview he said that everybody's crazy, and the person who looks like they are sane is probably the craziest of all. I think that's another way of saying the same thing that I was mentioning here about a sense of humour.

The reality is that as people we are weird. And it's better to just not try to hide all that weirdness, from ourselves or others. I tend to think that that is one way psychological problems develop — if we try to hide things from ourselves or others.

Well, this is hardly a new thought. Carl Jung said that suppressing an emotion doesn't work. It only pushes it under the surface, where it gathers even more energy and grows even more powerful.

* * *

But, speaking of growing and going under the surface, I think I should wrap up this episode. It's gotten longer than I thought it would. I was feeling quite tired after my full-day trip yesterday.

I was originally thinking of recording bits and pieces on the way, but I prefer to use this microphone, and it was in my suitcase, which of course I did not have access to during the journey.

So I ended up not making a podcast yesterday. That might

have been fun to do.

* * *

One other thing. I did not mention it in recommending the TV adaptation of "All Summer in a Day", but I did mean specifically the one from 1982. It occurred to me only later that there are also other adaptations, more recent ones. But I have not seen them, and I love this particular adaptation so much that I can't believe that anyone could do it better.

* * *

This was podcast number three, and Day 1 of 14 for my quarantine.

Thank you to everyone who has listened this far. I've received some very encouraging comments about the podcast, and I really appreciate it. It feels really good to know that there are people listening.

Thank you, and good night.

1.4 Day 2, Gratitude, and a Dream

Hello, and welcome to the fourth episode of my podcast.

This time I think I will make a change of pace. This will be a very brief episode, and it will be of a more personal nature, maybe.

I felt that the last episode was perhaps a little on the heavy side, going to these scientific studies of people watching films and the effects of entertainment and art, and segueing from that to David Lynch and the Dalai Lama.

This time I want to give a personal update and keep this more intimate.

* * *

First, this has been Day 2 of my 14-day quarantine. On Monday I will have my second food delivery in the time I've been back to Finland.

Second, I want to give thanks to the people who have commented on my podcast and given feedback.

It has been positive, and I have really appreciated hearing that — more than one person said that they find my voice and way of expressing myself soothing or calming, and I'm very glad to hear that.

That is a quality that is not necessarily to be found in many podcasts. I don't want this to feel like I'm pushing anything on anyone. I want it to be more like I'm talking to one person, so it can feel intimate, relaxing, and there's no pressure in listening.

I also mentioned in my first episode that I'm not going to try to make this such that everybody would keep listening. I'm not trying to "hook" anyone.

I prefer that any audience I may have consists of people who enjoy it for real and like hearing my thoughts and feelings and daily thoughts and experiences.

In the future I may also have other things, but for now that is the basic format. I also need to see about some possibilities.

Many thanks to my Polish friend Bart for your kind

comments; to Alessandra, in Italy, and all my best to your country in this terrible crisis, of course, that it is going through; to my game industry mentor and first boss in the gaming industry also, Maren, who also has been kind enough to listen to my podcasts and give very welcome feedback, and very encouraging feedback.

I really appreciate all your kind words.

Super thanks also to Norm Macdonald, my favourite comedian, whom I tagged in the episode where I was first discussing him and his comedy, and his style and approach. And he was kind enough to tweet something that made me feel very glad. When I saw his tweet, I was just about to embark on one of the two flights I needed to take on my return journey back to Finland from Iceland — described in my previous episodes — and I was feeling very depressed for many reasons.

So Norm's kind tweet really lifted my spirits, and it came at a time when I really needed that. He said something that I would be extremely happy to have as my epitaph one day. (Not that I hope that that day will come soon, you know — not trying to hint anything to the universe.) He said that I seemed like a fine soul. That really touched me, and I hope I'm worth that comment.

But whether I am or not, him doing the kindness of saying that to me — pretty much a complete unknown and a first-time podcaster who is finding his way in the dark using this medium that I'd never really considered up until just recently, when I realised that I need an outlet, a regular outlet for these thoughts and feelings and experiences, that just writing text on social media hasn't been giving me... Like I mentioned, it was an incredible lift, and I'm very grateful that he took the time to say those extremely kind words to me.

He has really helped me also through his comedy, in times when I really needed something to keep me going and to take my mind off worries. Norm Macdonald's comedy has really helped. And I'm far from the only one.

That's an incredible gift that a good comedian can give to the world: to actually make their lives better, and a little bit lighter. Or a lot lighter.

That's not escapism, either. That's a form of healing, or helping, really. But it's important that it comes quite naturally.

Of course, every comedian who cares about the art or craft — I remember Norm mentioning that he thinks of it more as a craft because you can figure out the process and the steps to produce a certain result, that the audience would be laughing as a result — I was saying that anybody who cares about the art or craft of course also does conscious evolving of that art or craft.

But there has to be a natural, spontaneous, organically evolving component to it, or it will feel fake, and as a result, it can't really have that effect.

I think that's an obstacle that keeps me from enjoying the comedy of many other comedians — who are fine people, who are following their own path and of course making many other people laugh.

But I really treasure this natural quality and this easygoing feeling that feels like he is really just enjoying himself.

I remember when Carl Reiner was on Norm Macdonald's video podcast *Norm Macdonald Live* — when Carl Reiner — a very famous comedian and entertainer and somebody who has done a lot for films and comedy — when he was on Norm Macdonald's first podcast series, he mentioned to Norm that he has this eternally wonderful smile — this great, real smile — out of any comedian that he could think of.

He was commenting on that, and that's true. You can really see when Norm is enjoying something. Which is most of the time he's doing comedy, on any of the clips I've seen on YouTube, for example.

And that's important. It's the same quality that Ray Bradbury pointed out you kind of have to have if you are creating something. He…

Because Ray Bradbury's advice was that if you are not enjoying what you are doing, for heaven's sake, find something else to do that you enjoy. If you are not enjoying the writing, for example, if you are a writer, then you are doing something wrong. Find something else to do, or another way to do it.

It's a sign from your subconscious that there is something that you are trying to do that isn't the right thing if it feels only like an uphill struggle.

Some things do take just hard work to put together. But if there's an enjoyment under it, then it's okay, you are not necessarily doing anything wrong.

But if it's always just pain and sweat and toil, then yes, that's not a way to live a life. At least I would think that a human being should be able to enjoy their life.

* * *

I realise that maybe I have been a little bit too systematic or logical, after all, in my podcasts. The way I have followed like a thread — that sometimes jumps to unexpected things. Still, my earlier episodes have been maybe more logical-seeming than I had intended.

Because I do want this podcast to be a journal also at the same time — a type of journal, where I can record things without that kind of feel of structure. And I want it to reflect the fact that my thoughts do jump from one place to another. Probably with some connection somewhere.

But so far my episodes haven't maybe reflected that. So I will maybe start experimenting with that more.

For example, right now I just want to describe a dream I had last night.

* * *

I have had more vivid dreams in recent times, over the last several months, than I've had in a long time. I know, basically, the reasons for that. Things in my own life. And of course now there's a whole shared world situation. So I can trace some of it.

I'm still very grateful for some of these dreams. Without going into this too much right now — into why I am interested in dreams — to say it as shortly as I can right now, it simply has to do with the fact that dreams are also experiences.

You experience the dreams and the things that happen in them. Just because they happen in your mind doesn't mean that the experience isn't real. And those experiences do have effects on you.

We of course all know that, because after a nightmare you're not feeling so great. After a happy dream you can wake up like floating on a cloud of happiness.

Last night was more like a dream that I felt was telling me something.

I don't wish to offer an interpretation of this dream. I only want to share the dream itself, or the most significant part of it. It was quite a long dream.

* * *

In the dream I was in an indoors area that was like a huge structure. It was a living space in that dream, but there were only three people present in the dream.

And I realised only after thinking about the dream after waking up that it was actually laid out like one of the two main malls in the areas of Iceland that I have been in so far.

I was with somebody that I know, walking on one of the

aisles. We were on the uppermost floor of that mall / living space.

And then there was a third person in a room situated in the aisle opposite to us, on the other side, across this dividing space. Occasionally you can cross over from one to the other by these walkways, but otherwise it's an open space between them.

Anyway, this other person was on the other side, and I was walking with this friend of mine on the other side.

She took off a diamond ring from her finger and gave it to me to keep, without the third person knowing about it. And she substituted a fake diamond ring on that finger.

I understood without words that she wanted me to keep the ring. She did not have to say anything, because I was reading the situation. So I simply pocketed the ring — put it in my pocket. And without that third person seeing.

And then the third person shouted from that room where he was — he shouted angrily to my friend about the fact that he was afraid of the dark and *she* had forgotten to turn on the lights. As if it were *her* duty to put on the lights. Because he's afraid of the dark.

And I couldn't believe that I was hearing this, and I just shook my head and looked at my friend, who went on to deal with the situation. That was the significant part of the dream.

* * *

I will wrap up this episode with this.

This was more almost of a check-in than an episode, although it seems I always end up talking more than I was thinking, before recording, that I would.

Again, many thanks for listening, whether you're listening now or a month from the time of recording or years in the distance.

Because these podcasts will be part of things that I am creating that will remain there, and that is one reason I feel this podcast is a more worthwhile use of my time than posting a lot only on social media, as text that soon sinks in the stream.

Again, many thanks for listening, and I wish you a very good night.

1.5 Day 4, Childhood, and the Future

Greetings, and welcome to the fifth episode of my podcast.

Today has been Day 4 of my 14-day quarantine. Today has been a day of low energy and low spirits. I've only messaged with one person, my friend Andrea, who is in the toughest-hit part of Italy, and I was glad to hear that he is doing okay considering the circumstances.

* * *

I slept a little bit earlier this evening, and when I woke up, I saw a flock of birds flying back and forth outside my window. At first I was thinking, "Could they be bats?"

But I guess not. And maybe I was affected by the fact that I had been listening to Norm Macdonald's brilliant new "Bat Song", which he just released yesterday on his official YouTube channel. It's a song written and performed by Josh Gardner, who also featured in the third episode of Norm Macdonald's video series called *Quarantined with Norm Macdonald*.

So there was this flock of birds flying around, and it occurred to me that I don't remember seeing any flock of birds before while in this apartment at the very heart of Tampere in Finland. Tampere is the second-largest city in Finland, and I currently live at the very heart of it. You couldn't get more downtown.

And my apartment looks into an inner courtyard, and when I opened my eyes when waking up from that nap — I'm not sure how long I slept — there was one single star twinkling between the Venetian blinds, in a clear sky.

"Star light, star bright.

I wish I may, I wish I might."

Don't we all, right now.

* * *

The other day I was talking with a friend about introversion and extroversion, and it occurred to me more clearly than I have been able to see it before that I think I'm more of an extrovert, actually, who was forced into an introverted lifestyle when I was young, after or at the age of 12.

I always remember my first 12 years as a mostly happy time. It felt like a happy childhood. I remember it as being sunny, and when I see photos of myself from that time, I'm always smiling.

But later events in my teen years led to me being without friends for most of my teens. And so, very important years.

And I only made new friends when I moved away from that small town in Finland and started university in a city called Jyväskylä here in Finland.

The reality is that everything in life builds on what went before. So those important years (if I have to count them, six or seven years after the age of 12) when people learn to socialise more independently than as children — I missed out on that.

I had discovered many of the things that set me apart from others. I was a nerd at a time when it wasn't cool, in a place where it most certainly wasn't cool.

The first TV series I remember really liking — feel free to

smile at this — was *Knight Rider*, featuring David Hasselhoff.

I liked it so much that I drew adaptations of the episodes as these comics where I used some kind of very thick record book with hard covers that I had found somewhere, and every other page had data printed on it, and the other side was empty. So I used the empty pages and drew full-page pictures, very quickly, not well at all — I was very young — when watching those episodes from video again. Or actually from memory, I think. I watched those again and again.

Anyway, I still remember from school, from those early years, that that led to others making fun of me. I remember there was maybe one person who admitted to also liking that series. One or two at most in my class. And the others laughed at it. It had a talking car that had many safety features. It could drive itself. I don't know exactly what their objections were.

But I think most of my classmates at that time were just reading Walt Disney comics. Donald Duck is very popular in Finland. I haven't read those comics in years, but I think that's what most of my friends were still interested in — at least out of the guys.

What's amusing, of course, is that these days many of those things that KITT could do in *Knight Rider* are actual features of cars. There are navigators that talk to you. You can't really have a conversation with your car, but it's still in that direction. There are safety features that help you drive, and self-driving cars of course are already on the table.

But I had also many other interests. I was into comics of many kinds. I read all kinds of comics. Superhero comics from Marvel and DC, but also these European comics like *Asterix, Lucky Luke*... There was a huge variety of stuff, really, that I read. *Peanuts* and obscure titles that few people would recognise.

Then I was into computer games, and also magazines about computer games. There were many great game magazines published in those days. That is a culture that has pretty much disappeared. Game magazines these days are like shadows of some of the inspirational stuff that was being done in magazine publishing back then, in the UK and somewhat also in the US.

But my favourite magazines, and ones that I had access to in that small town, were from the UK. They were published by Newsfield. And the one I followed because at that time it was the only one available — the others I only discovered later — but the one I followed was one called *Zzap! 64*.

And then I was into *Star Trek*. The original *Star Trek* could be seen where we lived only on a little portable black-and-white TV set because at that time that channel didn't have full coverage of Finland. But of course, maybe that added something to it, even, for me. Maybe it made my imagination work harder. Black and white is great. I love colour, too, of course. In later years I watched those same episodes in colour from VHS and then from DVD.

But I haven't followed *Star Trek* in a long time now. I'm not into the newer *Star Treks*, and I found many other interests, and now I don't remember when was the last time I watched *Star Trek*. It's not an active interest in that sense. And when it comes to the new *Star Treks*, they are not for me. I don't feel that they have what I would be looking for.

There's a problem that happens with any entertainment property that continues for long enough, and that certainly happened with *Star Trek*, already back in the 1990s.

The more you fill in detail and add detail into a story universe and the backgrounds and the things that happen between the characters, and more data about exactly what their pasts were, step by step — the more you fill in these holes that previously you could imagine — you could daydream about how their past was, you could add something to it yourself — the more you fill in that, which you almost inevitably have to do if you keep building it... and now there are hundreds of episodes of *Star Trek*, of course, and numerous movies, and they keep rebooting it, and so on and so on... and they keep adding to the mythology —

— but the more you do that, the less room there is to imagine anything.

The original *Star Trek* was good because it was like a theatre play, really, in look and feel. The characters had just enough detail and nuance that they and the rest of that world fired your imagination. It didn't do all the work for you. The sets are much like theatre sets, really. And I love theatre, as well as TV and films and everything else.

But these days it's so filled with mythology and continuity — a lot of it completely contradictory and inconsistent, of course — that there's no room to imagine anything.

I am curious — does any viewer of *Star Trek*, for example, or any of these other endless properties — do they actually feel that it fires their imagination? Because to me it seems impossible to get that reaction from watching them — the newer ones, where there's all this tight continuity and there's nothing left to imagine. But maybe that's something that only I and a minority of people are after, in any case. Maybe people don't want food for the imagination. Maybe they want everything done for them.

I prefer stories where there is stuff left to imagine. Where you don't know every single step of, for example, Captain

Kirk's past and education and every single relationship he had, and all this stuff that actually doesn't do anything for your imagination. It's like biographical detail. So it's like an endless roleplaying sourcebook.

* * *

Anyway, to return to my main point, the result of all this was that even though I have a great need for social interaction, and even though I believe that I am basically an extrovert — which may surprise some of my friends, who may think I'm very introverted — it's not that.

I have been working to escape the introverted lifestyle all along. And I feel I've made progress. My friend Amanda in London was kind enough to say that I didn't seem clumsy in my social interaction when we met, so far just once, in London, when I was living there for a short while last year. But it was definitely something that I've had to work at, because I didn't get the practice when I was young.

For example, I don't enjoy living alone, and that wouldn't be my choice. My ideal life would be living with someone — would be living a family life in a relationship and raising children, having all kinds of activities outside the house.

When I was young, I used to be very active. I didn't just sit in front of a computer playing games. That I also did, and yes, I also read comics and of course books — that goes without saying — and magazines, listened to music... but also I spent a lot of time outdoors, playing, having adventures, exploring, going to nature places, going outside — in the snow, in the summer...

I love sunlight. I went swimming. I used to go rollerskating when the rest of the town was still sleeping.

I still have fond memories of doing that, not because it was a happy time — it wasn't. That was the time, when I was doing the rollerskating, like at 4 a.m. in the morning, it was already the time when I had no friends.

But I remember the fresh morning air at that time of day. And I've found that the morning air smells different in every country — that I have been to, at least, so far.

At this point I have been to Sweden (very briefly many

years ago, just on a cruise) and then in recent years to Iceland, France (specifically Paris only), and the UK, where I have lived for a while in the London main area and then in Sidcup.

And I have never felt the same morning smell as in Finland in the summer when you wake up early and you go out or open a window. The air smells so beautiful and so fresh.

And I remember that and then going out on my rollerskates. There were usually no other people around. I rollerskated to the centre of town, about two kilometres away, and then circled back.

So I was active, and that's the kind of lifestyle I would enjoy. And that would be part of my ideal life. But many things are not so fun to do just by yourself. My situation is such that most of my friends are far away.

And another sign of extroversion in myself, I would say, is the fact that with the right person, I never tire of their company.

Also, when I was younger, I watched TV and films a lot of

the time — most of the time, I would say — with somebody else from my family. Sometimes with the whole family even. And so it was a social experience. And in recent years I have not watched so much TV or [so many] films, because I particularly miss the experience of watching with others — having the shared experience.

I watch a lot of stuff on YouTube every day, in particular when falling asleep. Norm Macdonald and things like clips from *Curb Your Enthusiasm*[9] feature prominently in my YouTube adventures.

But sitting down for entire films when having a solitary existence would not be my first choice. I would choose to live in such company that I could share the experience. And I have treasured the experience whenever I have gotten to do that in the past.

So most of the time, I do my own creative stuff instead, rather than watch a film or full episodes of a TV series, for example.

---

[9] A mark of the particular moment in time when I recorded this. I was watching more of the latter at this point than I've done since, at least so far.

* * *

Speaking of that, I might make an exception for *Curb Your Enthusiasm*, the Larry David series, because I find that that's one of the comedy series that I don't get tired of and that really, genuinely makes me laugh. It's so good.

I think it has almost the same relationship to… I think in some way you could almost compare *Curb Your Enthusiasm* with *Seinfeld*, which Larry David co-created and co-wrote for most of its run… as the third season of *Twin Peaks*, as compared to the first two seasons from the early 90s. *Curb Your Enthusiasm* and season 3 of *Twin Peaks* — they are the most heightened and extreme and — you can well say — most advanced versions of those creators' work. Larry David and David Lynch.

Because of course David Lynch directed all of season 3 of *Twin Peaks*, which was brilliant.

I'm not sure if many people realise, but from the first two seasons of *Twin Peaks*, David Lynch only directed a handful of episodes. His impact and influence was such that many people may imagine he directed all of them, but there were many other directors involved, many of them very talented, of course.

But every time when there was a David Lynch-directed episode, it went to a whole other level. Often scary places. Like really something that can give you anxiety.

But in some strange way, it's a good anxiety. Because it focuses your attention so sharply that you are not worrying about anything else in your life at that moment. And that is actually a healing thing. Because the brain gets a break from the worries that you may be obsessing over, when you are watching it.

But I don't want to stress this anxiety element so much, because like I mentioned in a previous episode of this podcast, there's also the light, and the fantastic humour that David Lynch also puts in there.

Like I was saying, maybe I should start watching *Curb Your Enthusiasm*, because actually I still have not watched the whole episodes. I haven't had a subscription to any service, for example, where I could watch all of them. But I know I will enjoy it, because I've enjoyed the vast majority of clips

I've watched from that series on YouTube.

Like for example nearly any scene between Larry David and Richard Lewis. Most of them are just great.

And there is no laugh track. It's also a special series in that there is only a loose storyline, a loose idea what each scene needs to achieve, and then most of it is usually improvised. It's not a fully scripted series.

That of course is something that can lead to mixed results, but I find that overwhelmingly the results are great. They're not doing it blindly, after all. Larry David has some little experience in this area.

Plus it's a comedy that is very courageous and doesn't hesitate to go into places where no one else could go. There are scenes and subject matter that you probably couldn't do if you were just starting out as a comedian. If you were not already established and if you didn't have a certain visibility and a track record, you couldn't probably start out with that material.

But of course Larry David earned the position — to be able

to do those things — with all his previous work. So that's a privilege that he worked for.

And in *Curb Your Enthusiasm* it's been taken very far indeed.

* * *

This was today's podcast. Random associations and a little bit about my background and where I hope my life may one day end up.

The happiest moments of my life have been spent in the company of another person. And my aim is not to be alone forever. That is not a happy life or outcome for me.

I don't see where the road can go that will lead me to my dreamed-of future. But I am still, in blind faith, taking the steps that may one day take me there.

Just before I travelled to Iceland now for this latest — and for the time being, last — until the world turns again and we can all have more freedom again — just before that I decided to get myself a driver's licence at last.

I didn't get one when I was younger, because I did not need it. I never lived more than two kilometres from the centre of town when I was younger, and I loved bicycling. I loved going places by bike and by walking and running and, you know, having some exercise.

I used to bicycle through every winter, even, in Finland, and very, very rarely had any kind of slip-up. I got very good at riding a bike in the winter. It's a skill you can learn — to read the road in front of you, or the conditions, and to be able to know — is there going to be, or likely to be, ice under that snow you see in front of you? And so on.

But yes, before this trip to Iceland I decided I want the driver's licence at last, because in my future I want the freedom to be able to drive also anywhere I would like. I asked my driving school here in Tampere for a very quick schedule — the fastest possible, in order to make it before my trip.

And so in a little over a month I did get it and did pass the final driving exam. And so I had the card before I left on my trip.

Or I should say I got a temporary piece of paper that already gives me the right to drive within continental Finland, but I will need the actual driver's licence, which I'm still waiting to arrive in the post, to drive in other countries, including the Nordic countries. I will be able to drive — as a Nordic citizen, I don't need an international driver's licence to drive in the other Nordic countries.

So if one day my life does go where I hope it can go and I will be heading into that life that I envision and am working towards, then I would already have the freedom now to drive my kids to school, and for us to go on outings wherever we would like — and that's a great thing.

And other things like that. That's a freedom I previously didn't have. But in one month and a few days I changed that part of my life, to have more choices open for me in the future.

* * *

And right now we are living in strange times, with limitations on our lives that we did not expect to be having at this point. But still the thing to do is to remember that this is only for now. Life will continue and *is* continuing, of course, already, while within these limitations for the time being.

But also, one day the world will open up again and then we can do more. That's a hopeful thought, and something to look forward to in these times when I'm sure that I'm not the only one feeling cut off and trying to reach out, in what ways I can, to other people out there.

* * *

And on that note, I again want to thank everyone who has listened to any of my podcasts. Also including my American friend Stephen Abbott — your kind words were very much appreciated.

And also thanks to my Argentinian friend Javier, who also was kind enough to listen and — I have really appreciated the fact that several people have commented on the relaxing nature of this, because that was one of my main goals. That this wouldn't be one of these podcasts where it's trying to sell you something — sell itself, all the time, and keep you hooked. For example Javier — he got it right away that I wasn't doing the things that so many other podcasts do, trying to buy you all the time — it's trying to manipulate you and use all kinds of tricks. And there's always music going, and it's fast-paced and edited to death.

So far I've been happiest with the editing of my fourth episode because I let more of the natural pacing remain. And I'm going to aim for that also in the future, so it doesn't become too much of a machine-gun delivery. I'm still learning — what is the best balance to do all those things.

* * *

And now that I remember, before I go, I wanted to finally say — because I did finally remember it, to actually mention it during an episode:

If you would like to send any audio message to me — it can be anything from a comment, feedback, thoughts on the topics I've raised, or something completely off the wall even — I would love to receive your messages.

Also, in the future, as things develop — and depending of course also on other people — I would love to be also talking with someone else in these episodes. I'm already putting the thought out there that I welcome the idea of having a chat during one of these episodes.

That's something I look forward to doing one day also.

* * *

This was episode 5, and I continue to think of all my friends, and my thoughts are with many people.

Take care of yourselves and stay safe. And I look forward to meeting you again, or for the first time, one day.

For now, good night and sleep well.

1.6 Change, Tweets, and Brevity

Greetings, and welcome to episode 1.6 of my podcast.

I hope that this evening, or day or morning or deep night, finds you and your loved ones well and happy.

Talking in yesterday's episode about my past so much felt strange because I have changed so much since those times, especially in the last five years. It felt like I was talking about another person when I was describing all these interests I had in childhood.

Some of them continue to this day in some form, but especially over the last five years I have almost completely changed in terms of my main interests and the things I spend my life doing.

Rather than the things that I was talking about in yesterday's episode, these days a lot of my time is spent on things related to music. Listening to music, learning about it, my "odyssey" through the history of recorded music, and of course writing my own.

With my discovery of Norm Macdonald in early 2019 I became even more keenly interested in comedy and started making new discoveries in that area. I think it's fair to say that I'm a tough audience when it comes to comedy. I find it hard to, for example, find sitcoms that I enjoy. *Seinfeld* is the only sitcom I have watched from beginning to end.

* * *

I also felt that yesterday's episode perhaps went on a little bit too long. Today I want to make another change-of-pace episode.

It occurred to me that it might be fun to have either an occasional or regular segment where I check out my Twitter and refer to interesting or amusing tweets I have seen.

* * *

Among the first people I followed was of course David Lynch, and yesterday he tweeted about the passing of Polish composer Krzysztof Penderecki, whose work has also appeared in David Lynch's film works. And he wrote:

"Dear Twitter Friends,

So sad to hear of the passing of Krzysztof Penderecki. Krzysztof Penderecki was one of the greatest composers of all time!!!"

—@DAVID_LYNCH, 30 March 2020

His work also appeared, of course, in Stanley Kubrick's *The Shining* and the horror film *The Exorcist*, which I still have not seen.

Out of David Lynch's work, it was used in *INLAND EMPIRE*,[10] *Wild at Heart*, and the third season of *Twin Peaks*.

Of course the composer had a huge amount of other work, but I'm mentioning these films because that is where most of us will likely have heard him.

* * *

Then my eye was caught by a tweet from English author and commentator Norman Lebrecht. Apologies if I mispronounced that name. It was a link to his blog, and it

---

[10] David Lynch prefers the title of this film to be fully capitalised.

read:

"Major haircut at Philadelphia Orch[estra]"

—@NLebrecht, 31 March 2020

And there's a picture of a conductor in front of the orchestra. The conductor has very short hair, so I was interested to hear if there had been a major haircut at the orchestra. I hoped to see "before" and "after" pictures.

But of course when I clicked on it, it turned out it was a story about a pay cut, not a haircut.

* * *

Then from actor Edward James Olmos — who is one of my very favourite actors, alongside people like Christopher Walken — Edward James Olmos posted a very heartfelt video message about the people bringing food to the table of the United States in this time — as in, of course, times before as well.

A lot of them are immigrant workers, and this tweet from Edward James Olmos has him addressing us and them directly — talking directly to the camera.

And he points out how not only the first responders and the healthcare workers and everyone else working to get us through this crisis, also the people picking the food, doing the actual work of harvesting and so on — they are the backbone of us as human beings, as a species.

Like others have pointed out, this crisis has made it clear who are the people that we really depend on — on whose good work our lives depend.

If the people bringing us the food, cleaning the streets, cleaning the places where we live and work, and of course the cooks, the waiters, these professions that unfortunately many people look down on — those are the most important professions of all.

Our being alive depends on them doing their work well. So they deserve our respect.

This reminds me, I wanted to comment on an aspect of Norm Macdonald's final — for now — stand-up appearance.

* * *

What struck me about that after watching it many times —
I think it's really brilliant, it's an instant classic — and what
also struck me about the bat song that he posted very
recently on his official YouTube channel…

One brilliant thing about that coronavirus stand-up and
the bat song is that even while he is making people laugh
about this, which we really badly need… I think this is
exactly what's needed, and as soon as we can.

Nobody's laughing at the victims. But in order for us to be
able to ease the tension, being able to laugh at something
related to this otherwise horrible topic — that is helpful.

And that is, for example, something that did not happen
after 9/11. And that morbid seriousness about it back then,
I believe, led to many wrong steps taken after that. Because
people were not able to get a sense of perspective about it,
and therefore there were steps taken that most likely made
things much worse than they would have been had cooler
heads prevailed.

But to return to my point about that set and the bat song: a brilliant thing about them is that while they are making people laugh also, which is badly needed, and it's really a helpful and healing thing — I'm using this word "healing" a lot in these podcasts, but I'm not using it lightly — that brilliant thing is that at the same time as he's making people laugh, he's also going through all the main points to know, the things that we need to know about coronavirus and protecting ourselves from it and taking the right precautions.

He refers to washing your hands, not touching your face, the need for distance, the inadvisability of being in such close quarters with other people — and that is why it was the last of his appearances for now, until this thing is over. But he — even that point he makes in a way that makes people laugh. It is ingenious to me.

Also in the bat song, which features him cooking what is supposedly bat — even in that one you see hand sanitiser — Purell. And he uses it at one point in the video. That's in a speeded-up segment of the video. You see him take a squirt of Purell and sanitise his hands with it — while preparing bat to eat.

And of course the song itself ends with the thought that because of this thing now, the "me" of the song is no longer going to eat bat.

Also about that song: it has a brilliant last couple of lines. It's the perfect ending to that song.

I mentioned this in a previous episode: the song was written and performed by Josh Gardner, and it features Norm Macdonald in the video.

* * *

Actually I think this is a good place to end this episode. I do recommend watching that video by Edward James Olmos. It's a great message, and when at the end he says, "Bless your hearts." —

— You know, that is something that, when he says that, he says it with all *his* heart.

He's an actor that I have liked ever since watching the

original *Miami Vice*. He was my favourite thing about that series. And then of course later he appeared in *Battlestar Galactica*, the version from the 2000s, in the main role.

And what's interesting is that he had creative control over those characters. Which is highly unusual in this kind of TV series format.

* * *

This was episode 1.6, and I hope that you are doing well. Thank you for listening, and wherever you are, good night.

1.7 First Message, Autism, and Always Possibilities

Greetings, and welcome to episode 1.7 of my podcast.

Today is a special episode because it features for the first time in this podcast series a contribution from a listener — an audio message where she comments on something I brought up in a previous episode.

I'll get to that after just a couple of bits of business first.

* * *

After listening back to the episodes after recording them, I noticed that I have one tendency I'm trying to steer in a better direction. That tendency is to start talking about something and making a point, and then moving on to another topic without actually finishing making the point.

For example, in an earlier episode I was talking about how it felt strange to look back and talk about the way I was as a kid and teenager and even in my early adulthood, because over the last five years in particular I've changed so much, and I ended up mentioning just one area of interest that had become far more prominent than any of the other, earlier interests I had in life, and many of which have receded into the background and are no longer active interests.

I mentioned only my great interest in music — exploring music, educating myself, opening up my horizons, and of course making music — writing it. But that's just one area, and I didn't even bring up my writing interests. Because I did start out as a writer, and I thought for many years that I would only be writing — that I would be a writer and that would be enough.

But over the years I discovered that it wasn't enough. I needed other activities as well, and to be creative and to explore many other areas. And I have found that all of these feed into each other and strengthen the others.

* * *

I'm still doing my 14-day quarantine, and today is Day 7. So once this day is over, I'll be at the halfway point.

* * *

But now I should let my guest talk. She sent a great contribution in the form of an audio message. My first ever message comes from Maren in Germany, who is a good friend.

I got to know her when she was my boss on three computer games that I wrote for and did other text work for, many years ago. She was my mentor in the game industry, and she gave me my first opportunities to write something for games.

Her message takes off from my comments in an earlier episode about how I feel that, looking back on my own life, I feel that I am most likely actually an extrovert who got forced or pushed into an introverted lifestyle for several years in my teens. And then — since then — I've been working to open up more, to reach out more, to be more socially able. Because I missed out on social activities in those important years in our teens when we start getting more independent and learn socialising on our own.

And now here is Maren. I will let her take the stage and

I'm figuratively handing her the microphone. So I won't interrupt her during this message. Here's Maren.

"Hey, Simo. As you said on your podcast, maybe someone wants to send a voice message…

There were two things that came to my mind when I listened to your podcast yesterday, and one was that you said that you missed out as a teenager on social interaction, and that this might have had a very deep impact.

And it reminded me on an article that I just read about autism, and that it is or was the understanding for a very, very long time — and still is — that autism comes with a lack of social interaction and social comprehension — that you can't read other faces and avoid eye contact and don't want to touch somebody.

And I've forgotten his name, but a scientist said that he had studied a lot of data and that he came to a very different conclusion, and this is that autism or people with autism have a lack of sorting data in the brain — which is proved and is known very widely — and this can also happen when you don't have autism.

And it is something that Paul has, who's very quickly very erschöpft — weary or tired of all information that is coming in, and his brain has difficulties with sorting out stuff that is not

134

important, like — I don't know if you can hear that, but in the background the washing machine makes a noise and the kids play with Lego and everything makes a noise and smells, and there are lights and stuff like that. And especially because of his hearing... lack? — well, it's not loss, but he has a hearing aid, and especially in larger groups with a lot of people chatting, this becomes very, very difficult, and he often needs a break and to refocus and to get some more energy again.

And it's something we also notice with our son Ivo, and that was the reason why I googled some things and, yeah, came across this article about autism.

I know a lot of small children have behaviours that resemble autism. For example, that they want a very specific way of things to happen, and things have to be the same every time. And if they change, yeah, it really upsets them, and we notice that with Ivo this is a lot, lot more than with our daughter Ida. And Paul's nephew has autism, so we were already a bit... so we know the topic and, yeah, always watch out for these things a bit more maybe than other parents.

And I don't think that Ivo has Asperger's or autism, but he has a very clear, different way of approaching and focusing and working with data and... I don't know what Reiz *— in German it's* Reiz.

Reiz[11] *is everything that you get with your senses."*

(child says something loudly in the background)

"And... okay, I really have to focus again on the article I read. Because this scientist said that he doesn't believe that people with autism in general have a lack of... no, not social interaction, but a lack of understanding social action and being able to use social interactions — but that he says due to this problem with processing sensual information or the huge amount of sensual information that we get every second, they tend to withdraw themselves from situations, and especially in ages where people learn how to interact with other people. And that this is the main reason why they have difficulties with social interactions. Not because their brain is not able to do this due to their special kind, special way how they work, but it is due to the lack of practice and due to the lack of learning in these very key phases in their life and in their development.

And he says that in his opinion, this knowledge could help to improve a lot of the social interaction with children with Asperger's. If we help them right from the beginning to learn how to cope with this enormous amount of sensual information, they don't have this overwhelming feeling and they don't withdraw

---

[11] "Stimulus".

themselves so much from situations and from interactions and from people in general. And this will lead to a much better understanding and reading of people and emotions.

And I really liked this article. I don't know if it's true or — "true" is maybe not the right word to say, because I don't think it is not true. I just think it really depends on the person itself, and for autism there are very... "Autism spectrum", I don't know if it's called in English as well? So there's a very wide range of this behaviour — how deeply you are affected and how much it affects your daily life.

But I thought this was very good to see and to hear — that it is a field where people still find ways how to improve the life of people with autism.

And it also gives an insight that these problems don't have to come with Asperger's or autism because every time someone misses out on these very important phases in their life where interaction with other people is a key learning in this development stage.

And yeah, this was something I had to think about yesterday when I listened to your podcast.

Many interesting comments and insights in this message. Apologies if there were any bad edits in this segment.

There was a glitch when I was processing this.

My own experience strongly supports the idea that this is not something that is necessarily fixed in stone. There is indeed this wide spectrum of autism and autistic behaviour. There are people for whom it is far more difficult to change, but then there are also many people for whom change is possible, even to a very great extent. And a lot depends on whether they get the practice.

I should mention a little bit about my background. I completed minor studies in psychology at university, but most of my learning in this area has come out of personal interest, both because these are questions that also I have had to consider in my own case and looking back at my own life and trying to of course move in a better direction, and also because I know people who are at least to some degree autistic or have Asperger's-type behaviours.

Again recapping what I said in an earlier episode, I feel like I started out as an extroverted child who had a happy childhood, and I don't remember social difficulties before the age of 12. But then because I missed out on those very important developing years where we usually get better at social interaction — we get thrown into situations where we interact with our peers without parents present, and many friendships form, and so on — I did miss out on a lot of that.

But since then I have — I continued to steadily work towards becoming better at it. And I'm not sure whether somebody who met me for the first time now — to what extent they could see traces of that quite extreme social awkwardness I used to have when I was younger.

I also used to be very nervous about talking to strangers, but that changed already in my 20s because I just decided I want that to change, and so I started opening up more. And it's something that happens through practice — not being nervous around other people and being able to be more relaxed about things.

In my own case, I approached doctors many, many years ago when I started having very extreme sleeping difficulties. They had already started around the age of 12 or 13.

There's a difficulty about making any definite conclusion about my past and the way I was then and the way I am now, because of course that was when puberty was starting and there are changes in the body, and so on — hormonal changes and others — and everyone starts having some kind of difficulties. I remember that I started having more difficulty sleeping around that time.

There was also an event at that time, when I was 12, about whose impact I can't really be sure. And when I say "impact" — it was a literal impact. I hit my head quite hard. And when I say "quite hard", I mean there was a situation where somebody bumped into me, through no fault of theirs, and my feet were swept off from under me and I took the blow fully on my forehead. The front of my head. Which hit the ground and absorbed the full impact.

So if you imagine my midriff, and pivoting around that, with your legs going up and your head going down — that's how hard I hit my head when I was at that age.

Now, many years later I started to question whether that might have had some effect on me. And I talked to doctors about it and asked to get some examinations done. But the only kind of examination they could do was an MRI — an MRI[12] picture, which only shows the structure of the brain and not what is happening in the brain.

So any changes that may have come about as a result of that, that might have explained my sleeping difficulties and other problems I was having, it wouldn't have been visible in an MRI picture. You only see the physical structure of the brain from that.

So that remains a matter of speculation — whether that had some effect on the way I was in my teens and just on my life from that point on. I'm just mentioning it because it's also one possible factor.

But whether my own challenges in connecting with people after that age and learning social interaction, becoming again more extroverted like I started out being — I think I can safely say that in my own case, I was able to make a great change.

---

[12] Magnetic Resonance Imaging. As a result of this and another scan at another time, of my spine, I have MRI pictures of both my brain and spine.

I remember still the time in my teens when I actually had to learn to keep eye contact. That might be something that's common in teenagers, but I think it was especially something — I became aware of all these things where I was kind of lost in my own world, because I was so isolated a lot of the time. So I had to consciously learn to keep eye contact, and not just, you know, look somewhere else when somebody was talking to me.

And when I was talking to the doctors about this possibility that hitting my head when I was young might have affected me quite deeply, the doctor who was evaluating me just based on conversations — he did say that there were some traits that might be described as typical to people with Asperger's. But I wasn't extreme enough to be diagnosed as Asperger's.

I used to have a way more black-and-white way of thinking. Like that things are either right or wrong. But that hasn't been true for some time now.

So that wasn't something that was inherent in me as a person, as an unchangeable trait. That was something I learned, and I still even remember the times when I was learning that kind of thinking, in my teens.

So some part of it was the social isolation, just being so much by myself. Some of it was that I decided, in a way, or had a tendency to go in the direction of wanting definite answers — that things need to be either this way or it's not right — being able to say that this is the right way to do something, and the other way would be wrong. There was no middle ground.

* * *

This was quite a heavy delve into my past, but I only wanted to talk in such detail about it to make it clear that I'm speaking from experience. And the difficulties I had in the past with social interaction I believe I have mostly gotten over at this point in my life.

I have of course no idea how I come across. I'm sure that there are still traces of that. But nothing about it — the way I was in the past — was impossible to change or fixed in stone.

Psychologists and doctors and so on used to believe, I think quite strongly, that once you become an adult, only very little change is possible, if at all. To me that's nonsense, based on my experience and what I have seen in other people.

To me, the reality is that we keep changing throughout our lives, and it's just a matter of whether we believe that we can change, and then start taking steps to change — or whether we indeed decide consciously or subconsciously, without thinking, to remain the same.

To me, none of the really good and happy things in my life in my adulthood would have happened if I had believed that that's how my life is going to always be. Because that was how it had been up to that point.

I already mentioned that I also know people who have at least traits of autism, that they have some autistic elements in their personality.

But that's a *description*. It's not something that needs to remain that way.

And when I say that, I say it because I do see, of course, the unhappiness it can also cause when people have so rigid ways of thinking or reacting. Because then they are not in charge of their own lives, really — if they are going along this track where they believe that they have the answers and other answers are wrong, or other opinions are wrong.

I think that's something that can only lead to unhappiness for the person him- or herself and other people that they interact with. Their family, their friends, their loved ones — everyone that their lives affect.

But also, very importantly, themselves.

And that's why if someone has autistic traits or Asperger's traits *and if* it is a part of their unhappiness or they are just not happy as people because there are these ways that restrict their thinking or ways of reacting, that is something that only increases my sympathy.

The change can only come from within the person herself or himself. It is not the business of anyone else to start changing another person. I think that's wrong. I hate all kinds of manipulation or attempts to change another person or to say that your opinions are invalid, unless it's like a very extreme case: of course there are some things that are always wrong and there aren't exceptions. I don't even want to mention them, but everyone can think of many examples of things that are never right.

But everything else in life falls somewhere in between, where there's no clear right or wrong. And because I myself, at this stage in my life — I don't think that I have all the right answers, and I do not think that I know better than anyone else.

The way I see it, all of us know some things better than other people or have a deeper understanding of them — but then that is true of everyone else also. No one is an expert in every area.

And the reason for change, of course, ultimately, or the motivation why somebody might choose to change and start working towards that is to live a happier life and one that can be more joyful and worth living. Both for the person themselves and others.

* * *

Those are my current thoughts on this. The reason I was going to such detail was to make it clear that I believe in the possibility of change, for everyone. Change for the better, happier, and less bound and controlled by our past selves and also others.

* * *

I hope I said something worth hearing or thinking about, but even if not, I hope that you have a happy day ahead, and before that, if you are going to sleep now, a very good night.

1.8 Odyssey, Adagio, and Back to Work

Greetings, and welcome to episode 1.8 of my podcast.

It is April the 6th in 2020. I hope that this week finds you well and healthy.

* * *

I took a few days off from my podcast to give both myself and listeners a small break, and I spent the weekend doing my own creative stuff, especially pushing forward my music — writing some new music as well as continuing to work on my system, which I started to create for myself when I was in Paris.

I lived in Paris for a while a few years ago, and that's where I started to really get systematic about my composing, because I realised that I needed to create something that would let me create music on a daily basis or whenever I would want. I wanted to be more productive.

And I continue to build that system every time I work on

some more music, and maybe I'll talk some more about that system later. But for now I wanted to just cover several different topics in this episode.

* * *

This is Day 11 of my 14-day quarantine, so Thursday is the last of the days, meaning that by Friday I'll be again free to move around and go to stores here, and so on.

Of course it doesn't mean that the risk is over, but I'll have fulfilled the requirement of staying in self-quarantine for 14 days after returning home from abroad.

* * *

I mentioned in an earlier podcast that I'm doing something that for lack of a better term I have started thinking of as my "odyssey" through the history of recorded music. And that's something I started to do when I got really serious about learning more about music and wanting to start creating some of my own.

What I mean by the "odyssey" is that there is this magazine being published in the UK to this day called *The*

Gramophone or just *Gramophone* — it has alternated between having or not having the definite article — it started publication in 1923 and has continued to this day, and even though today it only covers classical music, for the first several decades of its existence it covered all types of recorded music. So it is a great general guide to all types of music published in those decades when it covered every kind of music.

So a few years ago I started going through all of these issues. The number of issues hit 1,000 some years ago — I forget when exactly. I started going through them, because there is a digital archive — very affordable — that gives you access to all the back issues. The earliest issues don't have all the advertisements — the advertising pages. Fortunately the later ones do.

With that and Spotify, which is of course a great resource for music from all ages, I started widening my education even further. By that point my musical tastes were already quite diverse, because over the years I had gotten interested in ever more different types of music.

In the 80s I already started hearing all kinds of music from many different places: TV, computer games, films, just music by itself, and many other sources, of course.

In the late 90s I played a computer game series called *Atlantis*, a French computer game series of adventure games. It featured very high-quality, actually recorded music featuring instruments from all over the world. The first game had a soundtrack by Pierre Estève and Stéphane Picq, and the second one was all by Pierre Estève. And Pierre also returned for one of the later games in the series.

That was my big exposure to the sounds of different cultures, so that really opened up a whole new world for me.

And then it was only a few years after that when my interest in classical music — which had existed all along, but I hadn't really delved into it — that's when it really became something for me that I wanted to jump into. I went on eBay, and I purchased a complete collection of *BBC Music Magazine*, like the first ten volumes from 1992 onward.

And it had all the cover CDs, which featured full works of classical music — and often very good-quality performances. And I started reading, learning more, and I listened through all the CDs. And I have them to this day, and that magazine collection.

And then more years passed as I continued to, at that time, focus mainly on my writing, and then, I think it was about six years ago or something when I realised that actually I want to learn how to do this myself.

I had never been fortunate enough to go to music school, because where I grew up there weren't any music schools. There was just the regular primary school. And my few experiences with music in a school setting were unfortunately bad ones. We didn't really have a great music teacher at any point when I was in school.

To cut a long story short, it was only then, those maybe six years ago, when it just became irresistible.

* * *

But that's all I think I want to say about this topic today.

I'm aiming to make these episodes fairly short, to be able to do more of them and also to keep them nice and concise. With some exceptions, depending on the day, of course, and what I feel like talking about.

* * *

But speaking of *The Gramophone* magazine, just the other day I was reading the issue from March 1943, when of course the Second World War was still very much going, and that was when they first mention Samuel Barber's *Adagio for Strings*, which is a very famous piece, and it's been used in many films and all kinds of places, at this point in time. So there's a good chance that everyone listening to this has heard it at some point.

I'm mentioning this also because I came across an interesting podcast that you can listen to and/or download yourself. It features directors Oliver Stone and David Lynch discussing their use of that piece of music in their films. Because both of them used it in a prominent way in their films.

David Lynch did it first. He featured it in his first nonindependent film, *The Elephant Man*, in the final sequence, which is extremely beautiful and extremely touching. And if somebody can get through this film and that scene in particular without feeling more than a little moved, then there might be something really wrong.

In this podcast I came across, or this piece of radio — it's a National Public Radio recording from the early 2000s, and in that both directors comment on their use of that piece. Oliver Stone used it in his 1980s war film *Platoon* as, apparently, a kind of a theme tune. I haven't seen that film. And if you want to hear David Lynch's take on this, and Oliver Stone's, they both comment on how they came to use that piece of music for their films, and also they comment on the fact that it appeared in both of their films.

You can find this National Public Radio recording if you google *"NPR 100"*, *"Barber"*, *"Adagio for Strings"*, and *"David Lynch"*. It is a recording from March of 2000.

* * *

And just yesterday I was reading the issue from April 1943, and that's the first time they mention the song "As Time

Goes By" from the film *Casablanca*, which was filmed the year before, in 1942.

Back then it used to be the case that once a new song became popular, many bands, especially dance bands, used to make their own recordings, so I'm now listening to the first recordings that came out, of this song. It wasn't the case like today that there's first one specific performance — that, for example, appears in the film — that that comes out with the soundtrack or as a single, and then only later others do cover versions. Back then, in the 1940s, it was still the case that the official version would come out after all these competitors.

Of course that's a great bonus, because if it's a good song, you can find many different renditions of it, and often there are many good versions in addition to the original one.

* * *

I'll end this episode by quoting from a soldier who was fighting in the Second World War and stationed in India.

Somebody quoted this soldier in this issue of *Gramophone*.

To me this is another reminder of how even though many of us are feeling anxious and worried — with good reason, of course — we still have many things so much better than for example at the time of the Second World War, when people didn't have a choice about these things.

They couldn't affect what they were forced to do or what they had to experience, even if they were fortunate enough to stay at home in England (in this case, because the magazine is English). The Germans were still bombing London and other places in England. Nobody was safe — then either.

But to quote from this letter from this soldier, who had not even had access to a radio for a long time (it was called "wireless" in those days):

> "Feeling particularly despondent and hearing a gramophone spilling out good music, I invited myself into one of my officers' tents, where I could listen better to, and in quietude and full appreciation of, Mozart's serenade *Eine kleine Nachtmusik*. True, only the first two movements of same, and

that with a piece knocked from the record, but not sufficient to destroy the hurtful beauty of such perennially fresh music."

He continues:

"I do think, yes, I do *know* that beauty, whether in scene or sound, can be extremely hurtful, but as it hurts, it, at one and the same time, mollifies and heals. I feel better for having heard this great music, rendered by what was once a great orchestra."

We today have almost all the music of the world that we can access at the touch of a button or a tap of a touch screen. That doesn't mean, of course, that tragedies aren't happening, because they are. And this still needs to be taken seriously — the thing we are going through now, all over the world.

But it's also good to maintain perspective and to remain hopeful and appreciate, of course, the things we do have — and the things we will have again.

* * *

I wish you a very good week. I hope you will remain

healthy and well. And take care of yourself and your loved ones. Good night.

1.9 Last Day, Pekar, and Keys

Greetings, and welcome to episode 1.9 of my podcast.

Today is the 9th of April 2020, and I see a Finnish flag in the flagpole outside. That's because today is the day of the Finnish language. So I expect to receive greetings from all my friends, in Finnish, pronounced correctly.

I am just kidding. Finnish is one of the hardest languages to learn. Unless you happen to be born here.

* * *

Today is the last day of my 14-day quarantine after returning home from Iceland, where I went on a brief trip.

Like I mentioned in earlier episodes, I left on that trip before it became clear that it was better to avoid all travel. And when the Finnish government recommended all Finnish citizens with permanent residences here to return to Finland, then of course I started making arrangements to return. Tomorrow it will have been 14 days from that.

On a personal level, I can say that my concern and my thoughts are with people that I know who have pre-existing health conditions. I truly hope that they won't catch this thing.

* * *

Now I want to talk about other things.

I was taking a walk. It's a beautiful day here in Finland. On my walk my thoughts turned back to a guy called Harvey Pekar, who created an independent self-published comic book called *American Splendor* many years ago — decades ago. Quite a unique individual.

And while I didn't read his comics when I was younger — I was aware of them, but I have always had so many interests that every day is a choice between doing a few things, and of course that shuts out all the other things you could be doing (that's just life) — I was aware of him.

But only recently, when I was having a sleepless night, I went on YouTube and watched a collection of his appearances on David Letterman's talk show, from several decades ago. And this was still in the early days of the Letterman show. It was long before things got better for Harvey Pekar.

Harvey Pekar, what he did that was extraordinary was that he chronicled his own life and the lives of people that he knew — his co-workers and his friends and random strangers he encountered — and things that happened — he chronicled those things in his comic book, *American Splendor*.

And so, long before many of us started doing that online, via social media, to a greater or lesser extent, he was doing it in comic book form.

He was not getting rich by doing it. It was simply something he felt he needed to do, the same way any artist has a need to do certain things. He was not making a living from those comic books. He worked as a file clerk at a veterans' hospital. That was how he made a living. Creating the comic books was something he did because he felt he needed to — and wanted to.

In those early appearances on David Letterman — you can

find a complete collection of them on YouTube if you want — a very colourful character, a very difficult character, but that's not something I count against someone… In those appearances David Letterman treated him in a way that he later came to regret.

In those days — like I mentioned, it was long before things took a radical turn for the better for Harvey Pekar, in terms of his art and being known and recognised — and what Mr. Letterman did, to his later regret, was he made fun of Harvey Pekar in many ways. About his appearance, his behaviour — which of course could be very abrasive, but there are reasons for that — and Mr. Letterman even made fun of his comic books. And he did not see the potential or value in them — it seems.

That may not be entirely the case. Watching those interviews, I got the sense that Mr. Letterman was sensing that there's something there. But he couldn't quite see it, and he couldn't really see under the surface. He went the easy way of making fun when an opportunity arose. Even when the result was mean-spirited.

Both of them provoked the other at different points of these exchanges. But I think it's not unfair if I say that it seems to have gotten worse when Mr. Pekar realised that he was largely brought on to be made fun of, to be laughed at, like a village idiot of some kind.

That is maybe simplifying it a bit. And I don't mean to pretend to know really what was happening or the thoughts that were going through the two men's minds during those encounters. But Mr. Pekar did become aware that he was not being brought on out of respect for his work, but largely because he was a colourful figure and somebody that it was apparently easy for others to make fun of. But because he got paid, and because he did need to make a living, he continued making the appearances.

But without compromising his honest and very, very open attitude towards Mr. Letterman and these appearances.

I have to respect that when somebody can go on a talk show like this and not play the game *at all*. There are, of course, ways of not playing the game — the popularity game — that are not as prickly as Mr. Pekar. But still, it made for refreshing television.

And of course Mr. Letterman also did recognise that, and that's why he kept bringing Mr. Pekar back.

After these appearances, years passed, and in the end it happened that a film was made out of those comics, starring Paul Giamatti and other great actors.

It's a very well-respected film. I still have not seen it, just clips from it. But I look forward to seeing it one day. It's a quirky, inventive, and authentic adaptation of Harvey Pekar's life and the comic books he made.

And like I mentioned, Mr. Letterman did come in later years to regret how he treated Mr. Pekar. There was already a growing respect towards the end of some of those appearances, because at one point, after Mr. Pekar put Mr. Letterman on the cover of one of his comic books, chronicling his appearance on that show — when Mr. Letterman saw that issue, he later brought it up and showed it on his show, when Mr. Pekar was again being interviewed. And he was genuinely impressed and thanked Mr. Pekar for quoting him very, very accurately.

So it seemed that that was the beginning of Mr. Letterman's growing insight into the worth of what Mr. Pekar was doing.

I want to be honest about this: I have learned enough in life not to say that I *will* be one day reading these comics. Because I know that there are always — every day, doing one thing means not doing any of the countless — thousands, literally, and millions, literally — things that we could be doing. So I don't know whether my path will take me towards exploring those comic books later or not. I have so many things that I enjoy doing. My creative work and other things in my life are so compelling that I'm not sure I will get around to them.

But I definitely want to see the film, and it was refreshing to watch those interviews and to see those clips from the film. That's the kind of person that it is very rare to see on a talk show these days.

And of course credit must be given to Mr. Letterman for doing that, not only with Harvey Pekar but other people, especially in the early days. If I understand, it was more common for him to feature all kinds of people — people that other talk shows wouldn't invite as guests.

* * *

What I was saying just now about how every time we choose to do something means not doing any of the other things we might be doing with that time — that made me think of how incredibly precious it is when somebody chooses to spend time with another person.

Because it literally is one of the most valuable things that you can give to another person: spending time with someone else, when everyone knows that life *is* limited.

There won't be infinite moments in life, even though, of course, as young people we do feel that way. I know I felt that way. And of course, as years pass, that perception starts to change and we realise that it matters how we spend our time.

What could be more precious than sharing some of your life with another person?

* * *

Another topic I want to return to another time is also embodied in the symbol I use for my podcast — the key ring with the two musical keys. And that thing is keys to creativity, to put it very briefly.

I'm always, and I have been for as long as I remember, on the look-out for things that unlock something in me — that open up some horizon or make me see some possibilities that I was not aware of before. And I find that that is very rare when it comes to artists sharing their thoughts on creativity.

Many creative people can talk about their creative work, but only very few have that effect on me personally. I can only speak for myself. They may have that effect on other people. It's always about the combination of people and things.

But for me, just personally, only a small number of creative people have that effect on me — of giving me those moments of, "Yes! I understand! Why have I been holding myself back *this* way?" Or, "Why has my thinking been so restricted?" Or even, "Why did I forget this? Why did I start doing things in a more routine way when there are things like real inspiration and real insight that can help you find your way in life?"

And for me, some of the people whose words and creativity have been very helpful, who have contained these sparks that are like lifeblood for me, in a way — in a very real way — have been, for example, Ray Bradbury, composer Philip Glass, composer John Cage, actor Edward James Olmos, creator-owned comic book creator Paul Chadwick (the creator of a series called *Concrete*).

* * *

As always, I warmly welcome messages of any kind — of any kind of comment, joke, feedback, random observation, or anything else. Or even if you just want to say hi, I welcome messages from listeners.

* * *

Now my quarantine is coming to an end. It of course doesn't mean an end to the risk, for any of us.

* * *

To all listeners who have listened this far, I wish a relaxing and happy and healthy weekend or week ahead, depending on when you're listening.

I'm thinking of all my friends out there, whether I'm in touch with you or not. I look forward to seeing you again. Let's try to keep our spirits up in this strange situation that we still have to get through.

All the best, and good night.

1.10 H. P. Lovecraft: "Ex Oblivione"

Greetings. This is episode 1.10 of my podcast.

Rather than one of my usual episodes, today I thought I would share a reading of a short story I did a few years ago. The story is H. P. Lovecraft's "Ex Oblivione". (I'm pronouncing the title in the correct Latin way.) The reading and the sound design are both by me.

Listening to this recording, I hear that my voice is hoarse to begin with, and it takes me a few sentences to get going, but other than that, I'm quite happy with the reading. And actually, considering the story itself, the hoarseness at the start fits in, because that kind of hoarseness is typical for people living by themselves who don't get to talk a lot to other people.

It was night when I recorded this, and I was reading from a thick hardcover volume of Lovecraft's stories. So the page-turning sounds happened in real time.[13]

---

[13] The reading is a single take, unedited to correct anything.

Now I will leave you with the story. I hope that you enjoy it.

And good night and sweet dreams.

* * *

"Ex Oblivione"

by H. P. Lovecraft

When the last days were upon me, and the ugly trifles of existence began to drive me to madness like the small drops of water that torturers let fall ceaselessly upon one spot of their victim's body, I loved the irradiate refuge of sleep. In my dreams I found a little of the beauty I had vainly sought in life, and wandered through old gardens and enchanted woods.

Once when the wind was soft and scented I heard the south calling, and sailed endlessly and languorously under strange stars.

Once when the gentle rain fell I glided in a barge down a sunless stream under the earth till I reached another world of purple twilight, iridescent arbours, and undying roses.

And once I walked through a golden valley that led to shadowy groves and ruins, and ended in a mighty wall green with antique vines, and pierced by a little gate of bronze.

Many times I walked through that valley, and longer and longer would I pause in the spectral half-light where the giant trees squirmed and twisted grotesquely, and the grey ground stretched damply from trunk to trunk, sometimes disclosing the mould-stained stones of buried temples. And always the goal of my fancies was the mighty vine-grown wall with the little gate of bronze therein.

After a while, as the days of waking became less and less bearable from their greyness and sameness, I would often drift in opiate peace through the valley and the shadowy groves, and wonder how I might seize them for my eternal dwelling-place, so that I need no more crawl back to a dull world stript of interest and new colours. And so[14] as I looked upon the little gate in the mighty wall, I felt that beyond it lay a dream-country from which, once it was entered, there would be no return.

So each night in sleep I strove to find the hidden latch of the

---

[14] This word was actually unconsciously interjected by me during the reading.

gate in the ivied antique wall, though it was exceedingly well hidden. And I would tell myself that the realm beyond the wall was not more lasting merely, but more lovely and radiant as well.

Then one night in the dream-city of Zakarion[15] I found a yellowed papyrus filled with the thoughts of dream-sages who dwelt of old in that city, and who were too wise ever to be born in the waking world. Therein were written many things concerning the world of dream, and among them was lore of a golden valley and a sacred grove with temples, and a high wall pierced by a little bronze gate. When I saw this lore, I knew that it touched on the scenes I had haunted, and I therefore read long in the yellowed papyrus.

Some of the dream-sages wrote gorgeously of the wonders beyond the irrepassable gate, but others told of horror and disappointment. I knew not which to believe, yet longed more and more to cross forever into the unknown land; for doubt and secrecy are the lure of lures, and no new horror can be more terrible than the daily torture of the commonplace. So when I learned of the drug which would

---

[15] Seeing this name and considering my own middle name as well as certain themes, I felt it was only right to make this particular story my first Lovecraft reading.

unlock the gate and drive me through, I resolved to take it when next I awaked.

Last night I swallowed the drug and floated dreamily into the golden valley and the shadowy groves; and when I came this time to the antique wall, I saw that the small gate of bronze was ajar. From beyond came a glow that weirdly lit the giant twisted trees and the tops of the buried temples, and I drifted on songfully, expectant of the glories of the land from whence I should never return.

But as the gate swung wider and the sorcery of drug and dream pushed me through, I knew that all sights and glories were at an end; for in that new realm was neither land nor sea, but only the white void of unpeopled and illimitable space. So, happier than I had ever dared hoped to be, I dissolved again into that native infinity of crystal oblivion from which the daemon Life had called me for one brief and desolate hour.

1.11 More Keys, Encouragement, and Accents

Greetings, and welcome to episode 1.11 of my podcast.

Today I want to cover a lot of ground without taking up too much time, so I may proceed at a faster pace than usual.

On the other hand, I am still aiming to keep this relaxed and calm, which is one of the recurring pieces of feedback I have gotten from listeners, and for which I am very grateful. Several listeners have mentioned that they find these podcasts and my voice comforting and relaxing, and I am really grateful for that because that was one of the foremost aims I had — to create something of that kind of atmosphere.

So, this time I'm going to do one thing that I have been thinking of doing all along, which is to basically jump from one topic to another without even any kind of segue between them.

I find that, having taken such a long break between episodes recently — having gotten busy with other things I needed to be taking care of in my life — has left me with a surplus of things I have been thinking about and have had on my mind, with the idea of sharing them in this podcast.

* * *

First I want to mention that, typically to me, when I brought up the subject of keys of creativity in a recent podcast, and I listed several people whom I personally find helpful in terms of them saying or having said things, in discussing art and their own creativity, things that help me get some kind of insight on how to proceed with my own creativity —

(And that is, to me, extremely valuable, and I'm always — every day I'm on the hunt for things like this. And that is a big reason I value these certain people.)

— but what I started out saying is that, typically to me, I left out some really big names that I would put at the top of that list. Maybe it's that I have so many such inspirations, or maybe there's an inner saboteur that was kind of making me forget.

But I wanted to correct that mistake now by mentioning that maybe the three creators that have been most helpful to me in this way are David Lynch, the composer Vangelis, and another composer called Ron Jones — who used to compose for *Star Trek* a very long time ago, before being let go for, essentially, creating music that was too distinctive, too good, and too much of a voice in the overall product. Which is of course ridiculous, but I won't go more into that right now.

These are people whose interviews and talks and conversations that we have access to on YouTube and other places are full of insights that come from their hearts, that say enough but not too much, and they are things that point the way or open the way to something. And to me, like I mentioned before, that is actually rare.

Many people, of course, who are creative people — whether creating works of art or performing or in any kind of way — they can of course speak of what they do. But it may not translate into this kind of communication, at least for me. Maybe for others it does.

But yes, definitely, among the very most helpful things I have ever stumbled upon in my life — have involved David Lynch, Vangelis, and Ron Jones. I will likely return to all of these people, over time, in these podcasts, but right now I just wanted to get the names out there.

And each of these people is very unique. They aren't marching to anyone else's drum.

If I would just point out one avenue that someone might want to explore, it would be to look up interviews with Vangelis on YouTube.

He's someone who doesn't play the game of presenting himself as a marketable commodity. He is just himself when he's answering the questions. His thinking is so different from many musicians and performing artists, and so much healthier and wiser, it seems to me, that hearing those interviews was like a breath of fresh air. And even that seems to me like an understatement.

That is one of the most inspiring things for me always:

when somebody says something that you immediately recognise inside was something that you already, deep down, believed yourself but for some reason had not allowed yourself to really acknowledge — that that is how you see it also. Maybe because that way of seeing things is too unusual and you were afraid of others seeing you as strange, in a bad way, or conceited, or all these things that other people can bring to bear on you. Or, even, they can be imagined things that restrict who you can be, as a person or creative artist.

But then you hear something that suddenly just unlocks that something within, and that gives you a whole new path to explore or reminds you of something that you may have lost. Maybe you at one point were following that path, but then something got you lost on the way.

* * *

I was going to make this episode without segues, but this actually does bring me to maybe the most important point I want to make in this episode.

I was thinking yesterday of all the creative people I know.

People, for example, with great, beautiful voices, people who can sing or talk in a beautiful way or who can create music, who create visual art or write about art, or who write poems or stories… all these different things.

And it almost physically hurts me when someone I know and care about has so much potential, but they may be giving up on pursuing that road. Because things have been difficult, and perhaps because people around them are discouraging them.

It can be their own family, even their so-called friends, although I will say that nobody is really your friend if they are discouraging your creativity, or if they are making you feel like your dreams are stupid or that you are not worth those dreams.

If there's anyone like that around you, my advice is, get rid of them.

And I don't even care if it's your family members. You can first bring this up with them and see if they respect your request to not beat you down or try to discourage you or make you feel like you are not worth those dreams and achievements that you desire in your heart of hearts.

You can achieve all of those, in one form or another.

And on a more concrete note, I would say that if you can sing, or if you can act, or if you can record and you have a beautiful voice — if you can do those things, don't wait around for anyone to come give you permission or to give you a contract or to invite you to perform somewhere.

Make your own opportunities.

And if you have people around you, again, who don't want you to do those things, who are not supportive of your creativity, then those people are not your people. They are not on your side.

I just want to emphasise this because I have an intuition in several cases with people that I know that there are these limiting factors.

And that can even take the form of people you may believe are your friends because they are very kind to you in person, they smile at you, they welcome you to their home — but even that is no guarantee of anything.

Pay attention to what they support in the things you do —
or don't support. And pay attention to whether they really
seem happy for you and encourage your explorations
throughout life, and when it comes to also travelling and
being with other people. Because some people are very,
very, very good at being two-faced, and in reality they
don't really wish you to have success — because they
themselves are not having that in their lives.

That is a sad reality about human behaviour, but I think all
of us end up seeing it, over and over. And I hate that.

I'm not personally having anyone like that in my life at the
moment (but in the past I can think of some occasions),
and right now I am thinking of other people.

And so, again, if nobody is telling you — and again I just
wanted to put this out there in case even one person might
hear it who has been beaten down enough to give in, in
this area, or to give up — to give up their dreams of being
a singer or a performer or a poet or a storyteller because
people around them are seeking to control, in subtle ways
that may seem like caring, on the surface, or not wanting

you to get disappointed, and other excuses like that…

Discouragement takes so many forms. And don't take any of it, is my advice.

Let yourself shine and develop. That's what I hope for you. And I wanted to get that thought out there, again, here also.

I have said it to the people also in person when I have had the opportunity and that kind of talk has been welcome.

* * *

And again, despite my best attempt not to have segues, this topic brings me fairly neatly to another topic.

I was talking about people who can sing or whose voices are beautiful and that I think are even far more beautiful than any famous actor that I can think of — I know at least two people personally who have the most beautiful voices I have ever heard in my life, and ways of speaking and expressing themselves — and that reminded me of something I've been also meaning to mention in these podcasts, and that is that I think accents can be really beautiful.

Of course also people who speak their language in a native's fashion, born in that country and into that culture — the background doesn't matter — somebody born English can speak English also extremely beautifully, but I have an especial admiration, personally, for combinations of accents. For example, the combination of Icelandic and English can be very beautiful to me.

I used to have the idea, the unconsidered idea, I think, when I was younger — my aim was to speak English like a native of England or America — and it changed a little bit and sometimes it was — I was aiming for a mix of those.

But over the years I came to be ever more swayed in the direction of — why should I do that? Why aim for something that would make me sound like countless other people?

And the final clincher for me was when I heard English being spoken in an Icelandic accent. And then also just Icelandic being spoken. And that struck me as so beautiful a combination — of course it partly also depends on the person speaking — that made me realise that that combination could be among the most beautiful I have ever heard. And in that case it was also the person speaking.

But in terms of what I was talking about, it made me realise for good that it doesn't make sense to try to speak like a native of England, for example. Because if I ever achieved that, I would just sound like any number of other people. So I would have eliminated what it is about myself that is different from others.

And whether that's good or bad, it's not up to me to say, really — but like I said in one of those earliest episodes of this podcast, I think what we ultimately have to offer to the world, the thing that we can share, is only our own individuality.

So however our voice may be, that is what we *can* share of ourselves. And the way we speak — I think it's better if we speak in our own way.

I've even taken that into a place in my own thinking that I think most people studying English and wanting to be good at it wouldn't take it.

Because although I could speak in a very formal and very complex way and using fancy words, over time I started to see simple language as much better —

(Right there I could have said "preferable", but "better" says the same thing in a simple way, for example. But that's not a particularly good example of it.)

— when I also noticed that people who are not native speakers of English — they can sometimes use expressions that are lyrical and beautiful and memorable to a greater extent than something that would be called, like, perfect Queen's English.

That made me realise the beauty that can come of these combinations of languages and cultures and different ways of speaking and thinking.

I want to return to this topic also another time — there's a whole chapter I wanted to write in some book about the beauties of Icelandic, for example, because it reflects different ways of thinking than the ones reflected in

English, and the combination of those can be very poetic and evocative, to me at least.

And inspiring.

What I was explaining here, in my own usual way, is that when I realised that, that people using English in ways that somebody who was a prescriptive kind of thinker would call "ungrammatical" or so-called "poor" English — I definitely would not call poor or ungrammatical, because those expressions I'm thinking of and those ways of speaking were even more expressive than so-called perfect English would have been.

And I'm not saying this in any kind of condescending way — I really mean it, as someone who appreciates lyrical and unique and memorable uses of language.

And when I realised that speaking in a way where something may be a little "off" (so to speak — I mean it only in quotation marks, "off", because I don't see it in a judgemental way) —

— using language that way can be *better*, in ways that

matter to me, personally.

And that made me even start to sometimes use English, myself, in ways that — was less formal or that may come across as me not knowing how to say something, or not knowing a fancy word.

Actually it's more that I prefer to avoid fancy words at this point.

And I like the way comedians can use language, like Norm Macdonald, again, to mention my favourite comedian and someone who always makes me smile and even feel less lonely. Which is something that very few comedians or creative artists can do.

He uses often very simple language, but it's funny for that reason, and also expressive.

And so, while I could often go for a very technical way of expressing something, or to use an expression that features some jargon, I usually avoid that these days — even if I may then come across as somebody who is not so good at English.

In the end I think it is more important to let yourself be all the things that only you can be.

As long as you don't happen to be a complete jerk, and set on awful designs on the world.

I'm talking, of course, of people with some heart.

* * *

Well, I didn't cover as much ground as I wanted to. I ended up talking longer about these things than I had in mind. But I think there were some things worth saying there.

Just a couple of concluding thoughts.

* * *

I really like how people like talk show hosts and comedians have been doing "lo-fi" things that actually are often even nicer, in many ways, and more down-to-earth, more on a human level and less manufactured, than the things they had been doing prior to that. Not to put those other things down in any way.

But for example, Conan O'Brien is doing something called

"#Conan at Home", and yesterday I watched on YouTube his video chat with Russell Brand, and it ended up feeling like hanging out with these people.

Of course we are not really, but what I mean is, it created a sense of relaxation that usually doesn't come with watching actual talk show appearances filmed for television, which often are more structured and so on.

And because I, at least, have felt that a lot of entertainment has gotten so manufactured and so thoroughly designed and co-ordinated, I welcome this levelling down, in a way — bringing things back to a more human level.

And I think it's very refreshing seeing people just talking in real time without a specific agenda or something they've agreed in advance that they will talk about.

* * *

Finally, before I go, I wanted to say thank you to Andrew Mellor, who is a journalist, critic, and Nordic music specialist, and who mentioned after I had posted one or two episodes that he had listened to and enjoyed the podcast. I apologise for forgetting to also mention you in my brief lists of names earlier. I just have had a mind more like a sieve during this lockdown, I have noticed, than usually.

* * *

And now I want to get going. Just my words of encouragement and support to everyone.

Don't forget your dreams or let anyone speak you out of them. There are ways to make those things happen, and the important thing is to start making your own opportunities.

At this point in time, anyone living in our modern societies can, for example, get a microphone and start recording their own things and putting them up somewhere.

And anyone can publish a book on Amazon, for example, and that doesn't cost anything, either. So it's only a matter of doing it and getting those things out there.

* * *

That's all from me this time, and good night.

1.12 An Update, Dreams, and Hearing the Sea in Music

Hello, and welcome to my podcast episode 1.12.

It's the 28th of April 2020 — when we have 20/20 vision about our lives, in some ways.

* * *

Today I want to try something different again. My last attempt to speak without any segues was less than successful, and I want to try that again.

So this time I'm going to share a number of thoughts without any kind of link, like I tried the last time.

* * *

1. Today I was doing what I do most days, which is continue with my various creative works, which include working on my system of composition as well as of course creating new music, as well as writing, and that covers my work on screenplays and today, at least, on one non-fiction

book.

I don't want to share too much about these projects yet, because I find that that takes something out of the process — some magic. It's some kind of jinx that for some reason just happens.

I forget who I saw or rather heard mention this same thing, that if you talk too early too much about something you are creating, it is a kind of jinx. It somehow takes some energy out of it. Some magic. And then you make it more of an uphill struggle for yourself to finish.

So I'm avoiding that by not being too specific, although of course I very much look forward to sharing more when these projects are far enough along.

I mentioned that I'm continuing work on my system of composition, of composing music. And that is something that is necessary to do on a regular basis, because it involves building up resources and ways of doing things which will improve my ability to produce new music. I already have this set of methods and tools far along, but the nice thing about it is that it gets better and more useful all the time.

And part of this work is also being systematic with music I've written. Over the several years after I started teaching myself music, I've written literally tens of thousands of bars of music, and an important part of the process is archiving all of it and having it easily accessible for later reference, because a lot of it — when you return to music you've written in the past, you see new things you can do with it.

And some things, of course, are already finished pieces and are ready to go out. And with for example the Iceland symphony, which I will be publishing this year, many pieces are finished, and what remains is linking work and finalising some parts of it. And that is something I'm also continuing all the time.

And my aim is to be quite drastically productive in the future, and that's the aim of the whole work I've been doing on building my own system — my own vocabulary, when it comes to music.

One of my most exciting and thrilling discoveries when I

was setting on this path of composing music was when I realised that that is something you *can* do and that many composers do. I was reading about Philip Glass and how when he was starting out, at first he was writing more conventional pieces as he was continuing his music studies, but then at some point fairly early on he decided to start over and pretty much renounced the earlier work, as not being part of his mature output in his own style.

And what he did then was — he started with a clean slate and with the simplest elements of music, and he continued building from that, adding things to that vocabulary. And it kept building and building, and finally he had an enormous range of tools. As the years passed, it became bigger and bigger, so he was able to do more and more.

That is one thing that makes music so interesting. Namely how it is built of the simplest elements, and from those you can create endless combinations.

At one point I started doing the math of how many different combinations of just chord changes alone I could make from materials I have created for myself, and the figure became incredibly high very quickly.

I didn't write any figures down, but maybe I'll talk more about this another time.

* * *

2. I had a dream a while ago, a few nights ago, that had an interesting aspect, and it wasn't the first time I've experienced this.

In that dream I went to a downstairs, basement shop where they sold used books and comic books — the kind of place that it's not very clear will even survive after this crisis situation is over. But the kind of place also where I've spent quite a lot of time, especially in my earlier years.

And in that dream I went to the comics section, and there were Marvel and DC superhero comics, which I used to read all the time when I was younger. The modern ones, the actual comics, aren't even worth reading anymore. They are just something completely different than what they started out as.

Actually, the films these days are more worth spending

your time on than the comics that Marvel and DC have been putting out since the late 1990s.

Anyway, I'm not very invested in this world anymore, because I have moved on in terms of my interests. And other than watching the movies, which can be good fun — and especially in good company I've really enjoyed it, even though of course the stories are quite familiar to me because they recycle the stories I already read when I was younger…

But anyway, in this dream I picked up a Superman paperback, or it was a thing that we call an album in Finland. It's a format of comics that is larger in size — the page size is larger than regular comic book issues — and usually these albums have been like 68 pages or something like that. Not very thick.

And this was a Superman album from the 1980s, and the artist of both the cover and the story inside was José Luis García-López. And apologies if I mispronounced that.

And I flipped through the comic book in that dream, and I studied the artwork carefully, noticing details, and I especially stopped to look at two spreads.

One thing about this album that doesn't match how things usually were in the past in particular was that it seemed like the story was being told in full two-page spreads.

And on the first spread out of these two that I was looking at, there was a car careening out of control through some suburban or sparsely populated area where there were only some houses here and there.

And I turned the page, and Superman had been flying towards the car on that previous spread, and on this spread the angle was from the seashore, on the beach below this cliff, and the car drove perilously to the edge of the cliff, where it stopped, or it was not clear whether it was going to fall or not.

I studied that picture in detail, and I could tell the exact angle. It was where the water meets the beach. Then there was the beach, the cliff — and that went up some 20 metres perhaps — and then the car came halfway over the cliff and hung there. And Superman was flying towards the car.

And the interesting thing about this dream was that even though this was not a story I had ever read, and as far as I know, this particular story doesn't exist — it hasn't been printed anywhere — I studied the art in detail, and it wasn't a generalised impression of this artist's artwork — it was complete in every detail, down to the inking and the ink lines. And I really have a very vivid image of it — all the details and the way the shading worked and so on. And the way Superman was drawn, and — all of it.

So what is interesting about that to me is that my mind — and, I believe, all of our minds (I don't think it's just me) — are capable of producing new artwork in a style that is familiar to us, even though we haven't ever seen that piece of artwork before. Because it's a new piece.

And that's kind of staggering, when you think about it. The creative part of it exists. And of course even though I'm not able to bring that out by replicating that then on paper, it means that the imagination can create extensions of things we've already seen that are complete in every detail.

I'm somebody who used to really study the artwork in these comics, and I could tell different artists apart, and different inkers, as well as the pencillers — sometimes they were the same people, but often different — and even, at some point, the colourists, the people doing the colouring for the books — I became interested in that as well. And of course the writing was always of interest. But when I was younger I already developed an eye for recognising these different artists.

So here was a dream where my mind conjured up artwork created by this particular artist, José Luis García-López. And my mind was able to do, and I believe everyone's mind is able to do, this, even though lacking the technical ability to recreate that art in real life.

So the vision exists, or that faculty exists that could create that, and did create it, mentally.

It was really very clear, and that moment when I was looking at the pictures in the dream — it was an extended moment, it didn't just pass by in a flash — and the level of detail was complete. Not something giving a vague impression of that artist's work.

* * *

3. Here's a thought that had never occurred to me, but when I read it, it seemed to me definitely true, and that the person writing this had pinned down something quite interesting.

He was talking about how the music of Jean Sibelius — the most famous Finnish composer and actually one of the most respected symphonic composers in particular of the 20th century — how his music has a clear power to evoke nature — natural settings. In the case of his music it's forests and lakes and the sea. But in particular forests and lakes. And that's a reaction that has been shared by many, many people across time, and it seems to have come about very naturally and spontaneously. It doesn't even require someone else saying that here is something you can find in this music.

And the other part of that observation, and maybe even more interesting was that the music of inland composers — composers who have lived inland, not near the seashore, or not very often near lakes, for example, or rivers — there seems to be no suggestion of the sea, for example, at all in their music. And this applies even to some of the very greatest composers. This doesn't in any way diminish their stature or achievement, but it's a quality that I do miss in their music.

The inland composers that this writer mentioned in this old issue of *The Gramophone* magazine included Beethoven and Mozart. I have to say I feel it's true. I can't think of any piece of music by them where there's a sense of the sea — or even forest, actually.

But in particular, and maybe more definitely we can say that there's no sense of the sea in any music by Beethoven or Mozart.

A lot of it is either indoors music, designed with that in mind, but also in nature just reflecting more kind of indoors concerns.

Beethoven has a symphony that is called the *Pastoral*, and it is meant to evoke nature, but even in that I get no sense of the sea or any waterway — any body of water.

And this is an interesting thing, because of course there's nothing inherently reminiscent of the sea about the instruments of the symphony orchestras that Sibelius or Beethoven or Mozart used. They didn't use the exact same orchestra, of course. The orchestra was developing over time, and continues to develop, and now it can encompass any instrument whatsoever.

But so the suggestion of nature comes from a magical process of composition and involves this power to evoke impressions, without even these obvious ways to suggest waves, for example. It's somehow inherent in the music. Like, anyone who listens to the music of Sibelius, the symphonies in particular — it would be hard to imagine anyone doing that and not getting a sense of Finnish landscapes or forest landscapes in general.

* * *

4. Midsummer is approaching, and even though I have lived all my life in Finland, and even though Finland is the ideal country for celebrating Midsummer — we have

Midsummer bonfires by the lakeside and bright summer nights of often velvety magic — and so even though the setting is perfect, life has gone in such a way that to this day I have not gotten to enjoy a perfect Midsummer yet. In my adulthood, I mean.

I have particular ideas of what that would involve. The setting and — of course that would be a lakeside setting. And there would be rowing on the lake, and the bonfire, and staying in a cabin somewhere, of course. And more.

But maybe it's better not to talk too directly about your dreams. It's just something that occurred to me as I was considering how close we are already to May and then of course to June.

* * *

5. I was reminded by something — I'm not sure what — of something that happened two or three years ago.

I have still not seen the whole film [*The*] *Lion King*. It came about in the time when I was just a lot by myself, so I didn't have anyone to watch that film with. I would like to do so in good company, one day.

This anecdote relates to watching a scene from that film that of course is probably the most notorious scene, because it is the scene that is most likely to evoke tears in viewers.

Someone was going to show me that scene because we were talking about this type of scene that can have that effect on us.

Before watching that scene I warned her that I can't promise that I will be moved by it. Because I have quite a high resistance to scenes that on purpose aim to move you or touch you. I also need the scene to feel authentic and heartfelt. So I was just mentioning that I can't promise it will have that effect on me, but don't think that I'm uncaring if that turns out to be true.

Well, she showed me the scene from the laptop, and when she did, we were situated in such a way that she was at the computer, the laptop, and I was sitting a little behind her. So she wasn't looking at my expression in that moment.

But as the scene played out, sure enough, I got misty-eyed and one tear rolled down my cheek and onto her arm. And that was how she noticed that yes, the scene did make me cry.

There was no particular reason to mention this story now. It was just something I was thinking about.

But yes, I agree with something that Ray Bradbury said. This was in a video interview that you can find on YouTube. I think the video is entitled something like "Ray Bradbury on Love" (on the topic of love). And he said that a person who can't laugh, freely, is a sick person. Not well, he meant. And a person who can't cry — who can't release his tears, as he put it — is sick in that direction.

I would think that someone who has never been moved by any work of art to the point of tears, and maybe with a different work of art, or maybe the same one, to the point of laughter — real laughter, something they can't stop, they can't help laughing, or they can't help shedding a tear — I think that person would not be completely well.

Those are universal reactions. And they are signs of a

healthy person.

* * *

Well, that's it for me this evening, and may your day and night have some magic in it. I think we could all use that.

Here's to some better times ahead, and good night.

1.13 Simple Human Decency, Field of Dreams, and Some Humour

Greetings, and welcome to episode 1.13 of my podcast.

Today I really did not feel like recording an episode. The answer to the question, "When did I go to sleep last night?" would be that I went to sleep last night about 11 a.m. this morning.

And when I woke up after a few hours, I looked at myself in the mirror, and I looked like death warmed over — pale, red eyes, and so on. I thought there was no way I was going to record an episode today. I simply did not feel up to it, and my voice is probably not in the best shape right now. But I'm going to do my best.

When I woke up, I was exhausted and feeling totally wiped out, but as I slowly woke up, thoughts started coming, and before I knew it, I was writing them down as fast as I could, and I ended up writing several pages of notes. I usually have not had any notes prepared when recording these podcasts. I have usually talked off the top of my head. But this time I felt like I did not want to lose any of the thoughts.

So even though I would have preferred to sleep last night, at least the result of that and just getting a few hours of sleep was a sudden tumble of thoughts. So something happened creatively, and maybe that's just sometimes what it takes.

And now the problem I have is that I have so much I would like to talk about, and it will take a long time to cover this ground. I want to get to all the topics at some point or other.

Well, a good creative principle is that when any task starts to feel unwieldy, you can simply break it into smaller, more manageable chunks. And the smaller the chunks you break the overall task into — in other words, the more modular you can make it — the easier it is and the more freedom you have. The more freedom you give yourself.

So what I'm going to do is make a sort of serial — short episodes recorded in quick succession, maybe daily or every other day — and simply take things in small chunks.

One step at a time.

* * *

I think the real heroes in life are the people who keep life going no matter what. Even when it's the last thing they feel capable of doing at that moment.

It's not enough to manage that only on the good days.

The people that are real heroes in life are those who keep life going also on the bad days, also on the very worst days, and when the last thing you feel capable of doing is, for example, taking out the trash, or putting food on the table, or taking care of other things that must be done to keep life going. Those are the real heroes.

So in that spirit, or at least with that intention, I decided to record an episode today and get back to podcasting after about a week's break.

This planned quick succession of episodes is also more in line with my original plan for this podcast, which took as its main inspiration or guiding principle to be like a radio programme, something with a comforting regularity that you can tune in to and listen to whatever this guy in Finland might have on his mind this time.

* * *

When I was younger, I read a lot of superhero comics. And of course I thought because they were called superheroes that they must be the greatest heroes.

Well, I wasn't really thinking about it this analytically. I read them because they were fun.

But they were called superheroes. They weren't just heroes, they were super.

But as time passes, perspectives change, of course, and you start to see things from a different perspective.

If you consider for example Superman, the history of Superman, it seems like about 50% of the time he goes crazy and becomes a murderer or something, or drops his best friend Jimmy Olsen into the blowhole of a whale.

And when the whale blows it, Jimmy goes flying over the horizon. And Superman laughs, leaning back against some air molecules as he hovers there, and laughs.

Well, as far as I know, this isn't an existing Superman story. But I don't want to google it, because it just might be, from the old days.

And even today, about half the time it seems like Superman is turning evil. And when he's not doing that, when he's not throwing his best friend Jimmy Olsen into the blowhole of a whale, the other 48% of the time he is engaged in brawls and fistfights with some bad people, like a bad drunk who always ends up fighting with his peers.

And only about 2% of the time he's being a good son or potential future husband — pretending to be Santa Claus, or sitting down for a cup of coffee with his parents like a good son, and turning down a third cinnamon roll.

So, statistically we know from the evidence at hand, from all these stories, that about 50% of the time, about 50% of the days and nights, Superman throws Jimmy Olsen into the blowhole of a whale and Jimmy goes flying over the horizon, and most of the rest of the time he's fighting some bad people that he just doesn't know how to stay away from.

So Superman would be about the worst choice anyone could make for a husband. Unless one wants one's life to be a living hell of Jimmy stuck in a whale and flying over the horizon and daily fights with bad people.

And only 2% of the time turning down a third cinnamon roll.

Going crazy about 50% of the time is not good.

* * *

Well, in case this sounded like I've gone crazy, I haven't. This is just my sense of humour.

But my main point, which I'll now pivot into, is how these days I see simple human decency as the greatest thing in the world.

And a film that made me really see that for good in my life

was *Field of Dreams*, directed by Phil Alden Robinson, based on a book by W. P. Kinsella, and starring Kevin Costner.

* * *

A few years ago, someone asked me who my favourite actor is, or was. That question took me by surprise, and now that I look back on it, I think the reason it took me by surprise is that I don't think anyone had ever asked me that question before. Which sounds pathetic — that no one seems to have been interested enough to ask me who my favourite actor is.

Well, I don't actually really think in those terms. Usually it's more that I like a particular film or TV series or story in any other storytelling medium. So I don't really follow actors that way.

And because in that moment I was taken aback — I didn't know how to respond, suddenly I felt self-conscious — I didn't actually answer naming any of the people that I would put highest on my actor list — whom I appreciate the most. Those would include people like Edward James

Olmos and Christopher Walken and so on, but it's not like I follow their every film.

So I didn't really have a good answer to that, and because I didn't, yet I wanted to keep the conversation going and I felt like I needed to say something, what popped into my mind was *Field of Dreams* and Kevin Costner. So that's the answer I gave.

But the reality is I haven't seen many Kevin Costner films and he's not really someone I'm a fan of in particular.

It's more that at that point I had rediscovered this film that I had seen when I was younger, and I had spent a lot of time thinking about how that basic human decency that he was able to portray in that film had come to mean more to me than any kind of heroics — things that are considered usually hero stuff. Like superheroes fighting supervillains or that type of heroism.

I came to see that this most unassuming form of heroism is the type I really appreciate and value in life. It seems to be also the rarest form.

A lot of people do things for the wrong motives. Out of narcissism or desire to impress other people or to stand out in a selfish way...

The people who simply keep life going, who are good people, who provide for their family and make sure the home is a safe place where nobody needs to fear or live under a dark cloud when somebody gets angry — that's what I value most in life. And that's probably what gets the least attention when it comes to heroism.

The character that he plays in this film is called Ray Kinsella, and he has a humility and a gratitude at what he has in life, which is really the greatest treasure a person *can* have in this life: a happy, loving, healthy family.

That quality of course blossoms even further at the end, when he has worked through his issues and the simple pain of never having been able to say to his father that he's sorry for something he said.

At the heart of this film, its emotional core, is not a murder, and it's not a physical confrontation or assault, or any kind of physically violent occurrence.

It is simply the pain of having said something you regret and that you were never able to take back because the other person died. And it's too late for that.

And you are left to deal with that pain by yourself.

* * *

Well, this film is a story of a second chance, in more ways than one, and for more people than one.

It is very moving to me that a film can be made whose heart is simply having said something awful that you regret.

I can't think of another story like that. Certainly not one told with such humanity and, on the other hand, also genuine feeling. This kind of story would not work if it felt inauthentic.

* * *

Another facet of that diamond-hard pain of this character is his awareness that his father never got to see his grandchild born. He died before that.

This was an element that hit home also for some of the main people behind the film, since that was how it was with them too.

I know for my own part that I wish I could give my parents more than I have been able to so far.

* * *

I don't know how widely we realise that our parents go through literal trauma in raising a family. I don't think any of us realise that when we are young. But when we do, when we start to see the price they pay and how they go on from day to day to make the family get through it all, the very least we can do is give them respect and give back as much as we can.

* * *

Field of Dreams is a film that I never get tired of thinking about. It's very beautifully constructed, and it has a really exceptionally beautiful soundtrack by James Horner.

When James Horner was approached to write the music for this film, they showed the film to him in a theatre on a movie screen, without music, of course, or I think there may have been a temp score (a temporary score).[16]

And when the film was over, he didn't say anything, he just left the theatre. And the director thought, "Oh my god. He really hates the film. He's not going to do it."

But the reason he left the theatre was that he couldn't speak because it had moved him so much. And of course he went on to write the score, and I think it's his best one — at least the one that affects me the most, and the one I keep thinking about because of its simplicity and how it also takes its cue from the film itself.

Some of the people high up at the studio — they kept asking him to write a big symphonic score, but he felt that would have been all wrong. Because it's a personal story.

------

[16] There was. I thought I remembered the director and the composer mentioning that in the music extra I discuss in episode 1.15, but because I could not be 100% sure I remembered right while recording, I phrased this cautiously.

You don't write — at least if you have any sensitivity to storytelling and what is appropriate — you don't put in a huge orchestral score when you are telling a very personal story of personal pain and redemption.

At the end it builds up to more, and then it blossoms, but that's because that's appropriate at that point. Before that there are just a few instruments used, and it's completely enough.

This is one fascinating thing about writing film music. As in so many things, often less can be so much more.

* * *

I think the greatest people are those who, despite everything, despite whatever difficulty they may be facing on that day, or in the night, they still keep going and they do what is necessary to keep life going.

This is a crazy and unexpected time for many of us. And anyone who can act as a beacon of sanity, to whatever degree, or at least aim for that — I think that's a really good thing to do and aim for.

We don't need any more drama, and we don't need angry outbursts or outrage. I think most of all we need people who carry on. And not people throwing their best friend into the blowhole of a whale.

* * *

Thank you for listening and putting up with my strange sense of humour if you made it this far.

I wish you a very good night. Take care.

1.14 Trust, Darkness, and Ideals

Greetings, and welcome to episode 1.14 of my podcast.

If in the background you hear a motor sound, an engine sound, that's because someone was tuning a motorbike... Just a moment.

Yes, someone was tuning a motorbike in the parking lot of the building where I live, but I think they may have just ridden the bike into the distance. I hope so. It was getting a bit annoying.

But the day is sunny, and today I'm going to continue the train of thoughts started in the last episode a couple of days ago, and I'm going to continue unravelling the tumble of thoughts that came to me after I woke up that two days ago, along with some new thoughts thrown in that have occurred in the meantime.

As I mentioned before, this will be part of a kind of serial, so I will keep these episodes short and most likely do the next one in a couple of days and see how long it takes to get through these thoughts. After that, there are a couple of special subjects I want to tackle in episodes of their own.

But now to continue the line of thought from last time, when I was talking about the film *Field of Dreams*, which is one of my very favourite films.

Actually, let me backtrack just a little.

* * *

I really hate people who manipulate others for their own gain. Who are, for example, jealous of losing time to someone else, so they manipulate a mutual friend to see someone else in the worst light possible and play these kinds of games with other people.

I think I don't need to talk at length about what I'm referring to, because I think everyone has experience of that. This relates to *Field of Dreams* because I was talking last time about how I came to really value this story that has a main character who is simply a decent man — a good man.

And I had a somewhat ridiculous introduction to this

whole topic by talking about Superman — who, by the way, is actually one of my favourite superheroes, even though I don't spend a lot of time reading the comics anymore.

(Sometimes I go back to read some good stories, but otherwise I have so many other interests now that take precedence.)

* * *

Superman is meant to be the *best* man on Earth. He's supposed to be a completely goodhearted person.

A key part of that backstory is that he is an alien, he is from another planet, but he was raised by really good parents, really goodhearted people.

And that is why he ended up becoming one himself — growing up into a really good, genuinely good, person. And that's a valuable concept to me.

Many writers don't seem to know what to do with it, and that's why we have so many stories of Superman going crazy and all that other stuff.

But actually I don't want to spend now too much time talking about this. I was kind of just pointing out that there's a relevance to this idea of a good person, even though I wasn't even realising that when making that deadpan comparison in the last episode.

* * *

The connecting link between these things I've just been talking about to start this episode is, of course, whether you can trust someone or not.

To me, the most valued thing in life is knowing that you can really trust someone — that they are not two-faced, that they are not playing any game, that the reactions you get from them are real and genuine.

As years pass, it seems like such people get fewer and fewer. But of course it's just a case of people revealing their nature over time, through their actions, their words, and, for example, assumptions about others. It tells a lot about a person what they assume, either knowingly or unconsciously, about another person.

And the main character of *Field of Dreams* is someone who I think can be trusted completely. And not only on the good days. The key thing about the kind of person I mentioned that I admire most in real life and that to me represents the ideal more than these stories of superheroes, where nearly every superhero ends up being a very compromised conception, because there's so many people throwing in their ideas about them and it becomes a kind of a huge mess in the end, if you try to follow the comics, for example...

(Which I haven't since the late 90s, except for going back to read some of the really good older ones that had some innocence and value to them. When I say "innocence", I mean that that was the time before some people got the idea that superheroes need to be really dark and deal with the worst aspects of humanity and human life.)

And the sense I get of Ray Kinsella, Kevin Costner's character in that film, is that he would not start drinking or using drugs or something similar in a crisis. He is also absolutely not violent — which also is rarer than we may even realise.

Because — when we are younger, I think we don't have any idea how much happens behind closed doors.

* * *

There's a line in one of the early Sherlock Holmes stories — the short stories — where... I don't remember exactly if it was the case that Watson, Dr. Watson, was talking about the countryside in some kind of positive manner, or whether the subject just came up for some other reason, but Sherlock Holmes at that point kind of shocks Watson by saying that he has no romantic conception of the countryside, because to him, that is the place where terrible, evil deeds can continue year after year, undetected and unsuspected.

And that of course is how it is. Yes, evil deeds can also continue for year after year in the city. But I think it's worthwhile being realistic about it also that in isolated places abuse can seriously continue maybe for someone's whole life.

* * *

If there's one particular aspect of human behaviour that I hate enough that if it could be, if it could happen, if it could work that way, I would not mind that anyone who abuses another person would just disappear off the face of the earth, never to be heard of again. But of course that's not real life and it's more complicated than that.

* * *

Well, I started this episode quite darkly.

To circle back to *Field of Dreams*, which to me is a very sunny and of course very touching film… It also features scenes of twilight that are to me genuinely magical.

And I don't use that word too lightly. I use it fairly often, I have noticed, but I always have spent a long time thinking about that subject before using it of anything. I think it shouldn't be devalued.

* * *

Let me continue this train of thought after a short interlude here, because I noticed that I had written this down in my notes and I wanted to say it — because I think this is the kind of thing also that is useful to say out loud. I think sometimes that's something that can be helpful to hear…

So this is the thing. Even though I admire someone and all people who can keep life going no matter what… They are often, and have been often, mothers, fathers… The strong ones are the ones who keep life going no matter what. (Yes, I'm repeating myself here.) But even though that is true, that doesn't mean that they feel completely together. That's the key point.

Even if they are feeling very broken, they still find, somehow, ways to keep going and to, for example, lighten the mood or do something unexpected. This is, for example, one thing that makes me appreciate comedians that make me laugh. They often do so by saying something that is, in some estimation maybe, outrageous. (And I'm sure that some people would find ways to be offended and find some hidden motives that existed only in the perceiver's own mind.)

The thing is that — I for example have a sense of Norm Macdonald as a really goodhearted person. (I don't idolise anyone. I think I've lived long enough to realise that that's not a healthy attitude. I think being just a fan of someone, without seeing them as people... Everyone has both dark and light sides.) Having seen enough of him and seen enough clips and read about him, and being somewhat familiar, to the extent that it's possible from a distance — but he's very open, really, despite of course always having, or most of the time having, the comedy sort of between him and the audience — that's only sensible because he's a comedian...

But anything that breaks this obsession with feeling bad — well, obsession isn't the right word, because it's more of a reaction. But sometimes the reaction gets stuck, and we don't know how to break free of it. That's why the people who really just make us laugh — not by necessarily being crazy and doing some hyperactive antics — but someone who just kind of starts tickling your funny bone and you end up laughing and feeling better — that's really valuable. I'm still talking of the people who keep life going.

Anything that makes you feel more normal in situations that may not be at all normal, that may be very oppressive — that's helping. And it's healing.

So the part I mentioned that I wrote down yesterday or the day before was just this paragraph:

"Do I feel whole or completely together? No, of course not. I don't think many of us do. Isolation and loneliness are not easy things to deal with. That's not what a human life is supposed to be. Very few of us would choose it. And everyone more or less breaks down at some point. That's okay and completely normal. Let that happen. Let it happen and then, when you feel ready, pick up the pieces and continue again."

So just because someone keeps going, it doesn't mean that they feel perfect or that they are fully prepared for all eventualities. There's that saying that if you know how to bend (instead of pretending that you are unbreakable and nothing will affect you in any way), that is a strength, because then you don't snap.

* * *

And I don't think that Ray Kinsella, this main character in *Field of Dreams*, would ever snap. He at most would say something with a little bit of annoyance.

This happens once in the film. The financial difficulties of their situation are starting to weigh on him and his wife, and their daughter is saying something. And he snaps just a little bit at this young daughter of theirs.

But that's the worst that happens, and it's not like he starts yelling or going crazy or causing real fear in the kid.

And many people who may put on a good show of being really strong would not be able to carry on through the difficult times. Strength can be found often in unexpected places — and this is not, of course, an original thought to me. It's been said by many people in stories and elsewhere.

* * *

I'm looking at my notes again, so I'm partly reading here. I wrote so many pages yesterday and the day before in particular.

"The important thing is to keep going. One thing that is sure to worsen depression or anxiety is staying still and not doing anything.

"This continues the thought from the last episode, that the people who keep life going through good times and bad — the parents who find the strength to do that even though also sometimes feeling broken inside, and the sons and daughters, and brothers and sisters — those are the real heroes of this life.

"When the chips are down, those are the people who help us through. In the last episode I talked of *Field of Dreams* and how seeing that film again in adulthood, several years ago, for the first time since first seeing it just once in my teens, impressed me deeply in many ways, and not the least of those was with the realisation that in the unassuming and beautifully non-underlined nobility of the main character was portrayed something very rare and precious.

"It can be summed up in a few words, and those words are: a good man, or a good person. A person who with his wife provides for and takes care of his family, keeps life going." I'm partly repeating something I already said off the top of my head.

To continue reading from this:

"He's absolutely not violent. Part of the backstory of him and his wife Annie is that they grew up in the 60s and were part of the hippie generation, with all the ideals that entailed, and part of what interested the author of the book on which the film is based — the book is called *Shoeless Joe*, by W. P. Kinsella — and something that also interested the director, was the question of how the people who lived through the 60s and were involved in the working out of those ideals then dealt with and settled into life later."

And as a side note here that occurred to me as I was reading this:

This of course applies to also individual lives: how we start with idealism that fires us at some point, that inspires us, and then we have to find ways to fit those ideals into real

239

life. And some people don't manage to do that at all, or they just forget about the ideals. Some people manage to make them work when dealing with real-life questions, not some kind of hippie dream that doesn't really withstand contact with reality. (I say that with no condescension intended.)

To continue reading:

"The couple in *Field of Dreams* are in my view an example of a perfect adjustment into adulthood after the essentially teen dream of just flowers and making peace signs — which actually does nothing to create peace. That takes actual work. And it takes growing and maturing as a person to become someone who can be relied upon and trusted."

There's, by the way, a lovely humorous strain, also, to *Field of Dreams* that comes across already in the opening monologue where the main character introduces himself, talking about his past. At one point when he's talking about the 60s, he says that he, as part of this hippie kind of life, *tried* to like sitar music. I think that was a great writing touch and immediately conveyed something about the character.

Also by the way, that's an important point, because some people who try to act enlightened and project enlightenment — they would not admit it if they did not like for example Indian sitar music.

You don't have to like all kinds of music. There's nothing wrong with saying, for example, that you don't like sitar music.

This character, for example, gave it a try and didn't end up liking it. That's okay.

The honesty matters. It's quite bad if a person is acting enlightened and pretending to be into all the "correct", "enlightened" things, culturally and in terms of music and everything else.

This also relates to something I mentioned in one of the earliest episodes, which is that one reason that tells me that the Dalai Lama is the real thing is that he admits to sometimes breaking one of the monastic rules: he's not supposed to eat after a certain time in the evening or at night, but sometimes he sneaks out to get some cookies.

And someone who was trying to just project spiritual advancement or enlightenment or being wise would not admit that. They would just say, "Yes, I follow all the rules." Which would be a lie.

Again to continue reading:

"I was saying that he is non-violent and non-domineering. Violence, out-of-control anger, and controlling behaviour are always immature traits. No person who acts out such tendencies in his or her life is a mature person. Ray Kinsella is a calm man who can be depended upon. A thoroughly decent man who wouldn't crumble or start drinking in a crisis. Do we realise how rare that it is, and how admirable?" Again I partly repeated what I already said.

* * *

I have a temptation to keep going with this episode, but I'll stick to my plan, even though I wanted to get to other things already this time. I will get back to this soon.

Well, until next time, and like always, good night and take care.

1.15 *Spring Break,*
James Horner at the Piano, and Epilogue

Hello, and welcome to episode 1.15 of this podcast.

And to my surprise, I realised that it's time to end this season — season 1 of this podcast. So you have just started listening to the finale of season 1. I've been numbering these 1.x. For some reason, 15 felt like a good cut-off point.

I was going to continue and pursue the line of thought that started several days ago, earlier this week — I mentioned in previous episodes that a whole tumble of thoughts had suddenly occurred to me after an almost sleepless night, after a few hours of sleep, so it had some kind of creative, beneficial effect — but I think it was going to get a little too single-minded if I had just continued going by those notes I made. I still have several pages that I didn't really get to.

Single-mindedness can be a good thing when you are pursuing a single task. But life is not a single task. It's many tasks that come and go, and you have to pay attention to different things at different times.

And I felt maybe it's better if I throw these thoughts out the window, metaphorically speaking, and let the winds take them wherever they will. And the good ones I'll get around to anyway. They will come back in some form or another.

I wanted to talk about the film *Close Encounters of the Third Kind*, continuing on from this discussion about *Field of Dreams* from the last couple of episodes, but I thought it's better to maybe just take care of some clearing out of things in this finale and then just kick back a little and relax, and wind this season down.

I will continue with the first episode of the next season shortly.

* * *

Part of the reason I want to get off this more single-minded track for now and return to those things maybe later is that I ended up watching some things that got my thoughts going in very different directions again — reminding me of things I had not thought about for a little while.

One of these things was watching a great discussion featuring Philip Glass and Godfrey Reggio, the director of the *Qatsi* trilogy, for which Philip Glass wrote the music. This was one of those very refreshing creative discussions that I sometimes only briefly referred to, where the people involved say things that are creatively really inspiring, and they open up these vistas or make me see things that I don't always see. I don't always remember this, or these things.

The nature of *Koyaanisqatsi* and their work together in general was to present something but not tell you how to take it — how to interpret it — or what "message" to take away from it. They were concerned with creating something that left room for the audience.

So for example, they talk during this discussion — I'll post a link to it on Twitter (it's a link shared recently by Philip Glass's Twitter account) — they talk, for example, about how most music created for films is created with the purpose of telling you or directing you what to think or how to feel. And they didn't want to do that. They wanted to create an experience that would stir up things, but completing the work — to paraphrase them — would be up to the viewer.

I'm looking up the name of that discussion. *(typing on MacBook Pro)* It's called simply "A Conversation with Godfrey Reggio and Philip Glass", shared by an account called "WBUR CitySpace". But I'll share that link on Twitter also.

And it occurred to me while watching this discussion — there's a part where they show a little of *Koyaanisqatsi*, from a sequence called "The Grid" — when seeing that again, it just struck me how perfect a time this would be to watch that film. If you haven't seen it, or even if you have, I think it may make quite an impression.

But I don't want to say more than that, because I don't want to, either, be telling anyone what to think or how to react to it.

* * *

And another thing that I just watched before starting

recording this episode was a couple of clips from a series called *Northern Exposure*, from the 1990s. And it reminded me again in a very healthy way to also just mix up things a little bit more in my own life.

* * *

I mentioned I want to take care of a few loose threads when it comes to this discussion about *Field of Dreams*. One of them is that I want to say something that may sound like I'm contradicting what I was saying earlier, but it's not really contradictory.

I talked in the previous episode about how the main character in that film, who was someone who grew up in the 60s and was part of the hippie generation and whose limit of aggression was just saying something a little bit annoyed to his daughter — well, what I meant with that is that that's the limit of aggression within the family, where there's no need for more. But there are a couple of other points in the film that are not within the home or within the family, when dealing with other people.

The main point in particular is towards the end of the film, when someone is stepping over a certain line, where it's a matter of the well-being of his family. At that point he takes a stand, of course, because then it's a matter of defending. So it's not like he would stand by if somebody was attacking his family. There's a place for anger and aggressive behaviour, as long as it is contained and the person is in control of it, instead of the other way around, of that reaction, I mean.

* * *

Then a completely different point. There's a really great documentary that is also on YouTube. It's from the DVD extras, concerning the soundtrack and how that came about, and it features James Horner and the director, Phil Alden Robinson. It's called simply *"James Horner Discusses Field of Dreams"*.

There are some bonus features on DVDs and Blu-rays that I've watched many times over because I keep getting something from them. And in the case of this 12-minute documentary, nearly everything these two people say has been very influential in how I see things.

They are both very intuitive and creatively sharp people. The director has as much the right instincts about his work as James Horner does about — or, I'm sorry to say, did have — about his work. He of course is no longer alive.

And there's a respect between them and in their communication that I don't see between nearly all creative collaborators.

When James Horner sits at the piano and is playing some of the tunes they are talking about, if you look at the expression of the director, he's both in his inner world and also having complete respect for the music and the composer. He certainly doesn't interrupt. He listens.

And this may be partly me seeing something in it, but I think he's appreciating the moment, and to me it's no wonder, because the creation of music that is this simple on the surface but so strong that it's perfect and conjures up something, or many things, that I won't even try to put into words — I think that is very special.

I think it takes a special soul to create something with that kind of simplicity and beauty.

I could go on about this documentary and everything they talk about. There's one part in particular that I want to mention before I have to force myself to stop and move on.

At one point the director points out how a certain theme that plays during a key scene, where the main character along with Terence Mann (a character played by James Earl Jones) are driving at night, the director points out that that music is not any one single emotion. It depends on the viewer and how they are feeling what emotion they land on when hearing that music. So like the director says, it's neither sad nor happy.

Like I said, I could continue talking about this feature, but now I think it's time for me to kind of step back for a little bit.

* * *

I'm having this ginger-lemon or lemon-ginger infusion, recommended by my friend Javier from Argentina, and the reason I'm drinking it is that because I'm so much just by myself — that's how my daily life is right now — my voice can use some help. I don't get to use my voice a lot. So it's like a little boost before I start recording.

I hope that you may also have a moment to relax either when you're listening to this or afterwards — maybe have a nice warm drink. Or cold.

* * *

I'm looking at my notes to see if there's anything I want to still get into this season, before I finish episode 1.15.

There's a few dreams that I felt like mentioning or describing. They're from the last couple of weeks or so.

* * *

Either last night or the night before, I was dreaming that I was in some kind of store — I think it was a book store or game store or comics store, or something like that — and I got out, and I was with a friend. I got into a car with that friend, and we started driving.

I was in the front seat and she was in the back seat. It was somewhere between 6 and 7 p.m. on a Saturday, and I was thinking whether I should go back to that store — maybe I would like to do that. But I decided not to, that no, I don't need to, after all. It may have been closed already, but maybe not, because with this store, it's possible it was going to be open on a Saturday at this point still.

So we were in a car, and we were going downhill in a city. It was still light, so it was some kind of summer setting. And there was going to be an uphill slope in the distance, but right now we were going downhill.

And when I woke up, I realised that even though I was in the front seat and she was in the back seat, there was no wheel in front of me. *I* wasn't driving the car. At this point I have a driver's licence, so I *could* be driving. But she was driving the car, from the back seat, in that dream.

Later I wondered about this point, and it occurred to me that even though literally this could be described as "back seat driving", it wasn't that on a deeper level, because there was no dynamic like that. I wasn't feeling any anxiety about the driving, and I was completely comfortable with the situation. I didn't even give it a single thought, because I knew that she was a good driver. And she wasn't telling me anything, either — she wasn't telling me what to do, which of course is what is meant by back seat driving.

So it's a — it's an interesting thing. I think it had to do with trust and knowing someone so well that you don't even need to wonder about things like safety and so on. And there was a comfort there.

But it was an unusual way for a dream to express that, I guess.

* * *

Another dream I had, a longer time ago — it's been many days now:

It was some kind of anxiety dream, where there was a road and by the road was a waterway of some kind — a lake or something — and for some reason I wanted to take a shortcut or needed to take a shortcut. Maybe there was some construction going on, or some roadworks. And there were girders, these metal girders, set criss-crossing over the waterway.

And once I had gotten onto those girders and there wasn't more than two ways to go, to complete that shortcut and get across them back to the road, at that point I was with some other people.

And from both directions, along the girders, started approaching seals. And the seals were getting aggressive, and I was figuring out how to defend the people — react in that situation in such a way that everyone would be fine.

For this dream I don't have a particular interpretation. Maybe it will occur to me later. But it was memorable enough that I remembered it.

* * *

And the third dream I wanted to mention:

In this dream I was part of some kind of student group. We were all studying in some school.

It was a simple dream. A group of them just asked me,

would I like to go for a drink with them after the school day was done? And they would also give me and all of us — there would be a ride back at 1 a.m. or so at night, so then we could all just crash and go to sleep. Apparently we were all living somewhere in pretty much the same place.

I don't drink, but I felt good about the invitation. So I was wondering whether I should accept the invitation or just go to sleep even earlier. I wanted to accept, because I don't take that kind of invitation for granted. I would have, of course, appreciated socialising that way.

But on the other hand, of course, hanging out with people who are drinking, if you're not doing that, then it can be a little tiring.

Plus I was also just thinking of going to sleep, even in the dream. That's never a bad idea.

* * *

So I think this is it for season 1.

I want to thank everyone for listening. If you've listened to all the episodes, that's really great, and I'm glad. Or if you've even just listened to this one episode, I'm also glad.

If you didn't listen to the earlier ones, I could mention that I'm thinking of these as part of my legacy — the things that I leave behind. I feel it's more meaningful to do this than post these things on social media, where they will, of course, quickly sink in the stream. Those aren't places for things that you want to be found later.

I'm also working on several books and screenplays as well as my music, and some of the subject matter will overlap with this. But I like to think that there's some value in expressing your own thoughts and feelings in your own voice.

I have found that to be true of other people, at least. I am glad to hear people and the way they say things. It matters, and makes a difference. And every voice is unique.

* * *

If you're looking for a short story to read, I'd like to recommend one by Ray Bradbury.

Well, I'd like to recommend many by him, but at this

particular point, it's probably a good time to read a story called "The April Witch".

It's no longer April, but I think still of this time of year as spring. Maybe it's me being Finnish. It's quite summery here already, but not quite summer, so that's spring for me.

It's the kind of story that, after I read it for the first time a few years ago, I had the thought and reaction: "How could I stay for so long away from this beauty?" Meaning Ray Bradbury's writing.

How could I live a life where I was doing things and involved in pursuits where I wasn't getting certain things at all? I wasn't getting some of the most important things that remind me of what is important in life, and what isn't.

And it's kind of stunning to realise, when you have that experience, that it's possible to forget beauty and get lost in things that don't really give you things to go on — that don't nourish that part of you that makes life worth living.

That's really an interesting thing to think about. That there are things that get our attention and keep us focused on them, and we may even believe that we are really interested in them — but we don't actually get anything from them.

So we can follow, let's say, a TV series for year after year, and it doesn't even make us feel good. I don't mean in a simplistic way, like a fake kind of "feel-good" thing where it's just not authentic. But I mean where it at most leaves you wanting to see another episode, so the series is only creating a need to see *another* episode. It's not just sharing something and then letting you get on with life, like for example *Northern Exposure* does. It doesn't use this strategy of forcing you to watch another one, which is usually done in a manipulative way.

But I don't want to get into this heavy stuff now again, because I'm wrapping up this episode, and I kind of wonder if I should edit this part out. But I won't. I think it's maybe better let this episode be as messy as it turned out to be.

* * *

I look forward to some sunnier topics, also, next season,

and I'm sure that there was a lot that I forgot to say.

But the main thing is, the main thing I want to say is, that even though life is difficult, I'm sure for all of us — everyone I've talked with has said more or less the same thing, that we are living through strange times — I'm glad we're still all here.

Those of you that I have known for longer, I'm glad to know.

Those I'm not in contact with may have meant more to me than I can put in words, so I won't try. I will just quickly mention it in passing.

And those of you who I may not have talked with personally or that I haven't met — yet — I'm also glad to know you.

I'm glad you're out there and doing your things.

And I hope that you've gotten something positive from these episodes.

* * *

This season 1 was a kind of pilot season, in my mind. I was getting a sense of certain things and seeing how different things feel.

* * *

Just one more thing before I go. Remember fire safety.

When you are warming stuff up in the oven using that baking paper (I'm just mentioning one thing that occurred to me), not all of those baking papers withstand the same amount of heat. Check out the packaging.

And make sure that baking paper doesn't touch the edges of the oven — the walls of the oven, I mean — or the actual heating elements.

It's not meant to. You have to fold it.

Yes, this was a little bit random, but I just felt I needed to say it. It was something I needed to think about today.

I can imagine all too vividly what would happen if the worst happened in that situation and a fire started in an oven. That's just me.

Well, be safe, good night, and take care.

About Me

I'm a Finnish writer, composer, podcaster, and translator. I've lived in Finland, Iceland, Paris, and the UK.

I dream of a happy life in a warm house on a hill somewhere with the right person and a family in a life full of creativity and activities. Right now life is strange, but that's another story and not one to be told here. I'm going on regardless in blind faith.

In addition to this series, at the time of writing, here in 2020 (hello, dear reader of the future — I hope you live in a better time), I'm just starting my 6-volume series of books and its associated podcast called As Fresh as *Northern Exposure*, about the TV series Northern Exposure *(1990–1995)*.

My podcasts are on Spotify, Apple Podcasts, and rss.com/podcasts/simo. My website is simosakariaaltonen.com. And you can connect with me on Twitter, Facebook, and LinkedIn.

www.ingramcontent.com/pod-product-compliance
Lightning Source LLC
Chambersburg PA
CBHW021353210526
45463CB00001B/92